Mária Hári on Conductive Pedagogy

Mária Hári on Conductive Pedagogy

Edited by

Gillian Maguire and Andrew Sutton

Birmingham

Foundation for Conductive Education

Published by
The Foundation for Conductive Education
Cannon Hill House
Russell Road
Moseley
Birmingham B13 8RD
United Kingdom

www.conductive-education.org.
foundation@conductive-education.org

Second impression 2005

Printed by Call Print, Birmingham, UK

ISBN 1-897588-24-0

'Love is not enough here. It must be an intelligent love'

Mária Hári, *Standing up for Joe*, BBC 1, 1 April 1986

Wallingford, 1970   Photo: A.Loring

Mária Hári

from whom we can still learn

Contents

Preface 9

Mária Hári in time, cause and context 11

Translation, terminology and statistics 23

1. Introducing conductive pedagogy, 1968 29

2. A psycho-pedagogy, 1968 45

3. The great and the good, 1970 55

4. Exasperation, 1981 65

5. Out East, 1981 73

6. On the back foot, 1990 81

7. Diplomacy, 1997 97

8. Bowing out, 2000 105

The struggle continues 113

Index 115

Preface

This small book is the editors' celebration of someone whose contribution to Conductive Education can sometimes seem singularly unsung. Three themes stand out, the central principles of conductive pedagogy, the absolute necessity of appropriate professional training and her struggle against widespread and persistent misunderstanding of this essentially psycho-pedagogic system.

Mária Hári's texts presented here represent unpublished materials from the collection of Conductive Education materials held in the National Library of Conductive Education. Without the resources that the Foundation for Conductive Education directed over the years to supporting the bibliographic work of its National Library of Conductive Education this book would have not been possible nor could it have been completed in its present form without the individual contributions of Jon Bounds, Elliot Clifton, Anita Loring, Anna-Marie McGee, Emma Aldobolyi McDowell, Tünde Rozsahegyi, Erzsébet Szentesi and Jill Wilson.

Mária Hári in time, cause and context

Mária Jozefa Hári was Hungary's most extensive articulator of András Pető's Conductive Education. Even so, like the many conductors who qualified from the professional training course that she inaugurated in Budapest, she published little on the actual pedagogy, which is the defining feature of what the world now calls Conductive Education.

Lack of an articulate account of conductive pedagogy from an original Hungarian source has been a major problem in the spread of Conductive Education across the world. Those involved in professional training have lacked an authoritative basic text and those who advocate Conductive Education, struggle to establish conductive centres and defend them, or simply look in from outside and try to understand this new approach to special education and rehabilitation, have all had their jobs made the harder for lack of a simple brief overview. No wonder that misunderstandings and mis-statements of the 'principles of Conductive Education' have persisted over the decades, shaping perceptions of Conductive Education by friend and foe alike and taking new flight and apparent legitimacy in the twenty-first century as they spread across the Internet.

This book aims to close some of this gap. Conductor-training at the National Institute of Conductive Education in Birmingham, England adopted from the outset the same core of supervised practice as marked conductor-training in Budapest. From the outset, however, it also aimed to establish 'graduateness', which requires written texts. A persistent issue has been that the core subject of conductive pedagogy has had to depend largely for its written sources upon selected passages from wider texts and upon fragmentary materials. Conductive Education with adults enjoys the benefit of a major text[1] and there is an elaborated account of an untypical conductive practice with the families of very young

[1]Brown, M. and Mikula-Toth, A. (1997) *Adult Conductive Education*. Cheltenham: Stanley Thornes.

children[2] but for what has been a central topic of interest for many years, conductive pedagogy for children of kindergarten- and school-age, there has been little in English to present a principled, practical account of conductive pedagogy. The widely consulted book *Conductive Education* [3] has done little to fill this gap.

True, over the years the emerging system of Conductive Education has generated a considerable literature written by outsiders. The problem for those less than fully aware of the nature of conductive pedagogy is how to distinguish the nub of relevant, even excellent material within this ever-expanding corpus from the wrong, the ignorant and even the downright anti-conductive. Astonishingly, even after forty years of professional writing on Conductive Education – not least by those trying to practise it and to train others to do so – there are swathes of published materials, not just in English, which make no mention at all of conductive pedagogy as the vital factor in implementing an education that is conductive. Indeed, there remain many who appear altogether unaware that in seeking to implement an education without its pedagogy they are attempting *Hamlet* without the Prince.

Mária Hári's unpublished papers

Amongst the many materials collected over the years by the National Library of Conductive Education are twenty-four unpublished papers by Mária Hári. This is a serendipity collection, in many cases copies of manuscripts presented by Mária Hári as occasion arose to one of the present editors (AS). No claim is made that these twenty-four papers represent the bulk of her unpublished material that may well exist elsewhere, and certainly not – because of the circumstances in which much of this little collection was acquired – that it is representative of *all* her writing, her teaching and her thinking as a whole. Most of this collection is written in English, one paper is in French, another in Russian. There is nothing in Hungarian. Perhaps surprisingly, given the

---

[2] Ákos, K. and Ákos, M. (1991) *Dina*. Birmingham and Ulm: Foundation for Conductive Education and Alabanda-Verlag.
[3] Hári, M. and Ákos, K. (1988) *Conductive Education*. London: Routledge.

breadth of her involvement and interest in Conductive Education over more than half a century, nor is there anything on very young children and their parents, or on adults.

The focus of these papers is upon children of kindergarten and school age.

Sifted, translated, edited and annotated this small collection holds the potential to create a useful text on Conductive Education, but many of the original papers were too fragmentary, too unprepared, to go forward to a general readership without some rewriting, which of course runs the risk of burying the original voice of Mária Hári. In the end eight of the original twenty-four have been selected, meeting the criteria that they shed light on conductive practice and/or theory and have been available till now, if at all, only as carbon- or photocopies or within a very limited circulation. Of these eight, seven are the written texts of conference papers while one was written for a publication in a journal but not published.

The eight papers have been subject to varying degrees of editing. In some cases this is no more than any editor would make to improve expression and punctuation and fit together texts taken from very different contexts into a coherent whole. In other cases editing was more extensive, sometimes very much so. Another task was translation. In the case of two originally non-English papers this task was obvious. Some others, however, even though written originally in English or at least translated into English in Hungary, also required 'translating' into contemporary English to render them wholly intelligible to modern readers.

Along the way we may not always have caught the authentic voice of Mária Hári that many will fondly recall. Those who knew her well will still spot the occasional 'Hári-ism' – for example 'the contact' which has now entered the English technical conductive lexicon – and her very French-sounding use of the pronoun 'one'. Even though the text may not always sound exactly like her when she spoke English, however, we hope that the sense and the sentiment of what she was saying have been faithfully conveyed. Granting this, one often used to say that Mária Hári's explanations were crystal-clear, as long as one already understood what she was saying. If not, then her listeners might well remain little or none the wiser. To no little degree this was because much of what she was explaining was self-evident as long as one already thought within the conductive paradigm, the issues being further clouded to outsiders by problems of terminology and translation. To help readers bridge the gap a brief explanatory note follows this introduction.

The historical dimension

These papers can be read, individually or collectively, simply as Mária Hári's formulations and reports on conductive pedagogy and its professional preparation. To do so is interesting and valuable but there is an important dimension to this body of work, to avoid which is to miss an important critical issue: the historical dimension.

The materials presented in this book cover a span of thirty-two years, longer than the professional careers of many of its readers. Over that time there were considerable changes in the circumstances in which conductive pedagogy was provided, in the world's understanding (and Mária Hári's recognition of this) and in all of our societies – not least in Hungarian society. Against the background of these momentous changes each of these papers was prepared and presented within a particular personal circumstance, not just the common human situation of preparing for a conference but for Mária Hári – for whom the 'personal' was almost always subordinated to her life goal of sustaining and protecting András Pető's heritage – to meet the particular strategic or practical priorities as she saw them at given points in this continuous struggle.

Attempt has therefore been made to contextualise each of the eight papers presented here, drawing upon sparse written records supplemented by personal recollections. Mária Hári produced no explicitly autobiographical account, the nearest being where her *History of Conductive Pedagogy*[4] meanders across her own

---

[4] Hári, M. (2001) *The history of conductive pedagogy*. Budapest: International Pető Institute.

personal path. The introductory notes presented here cannot therefore state with certainty her mood and her aims at the particular points in a long career that each paper represents. They can at best offer presently knowable circumstance, leaving it to readers to draw their own conclusions.

Mária Hári was born in 1923. Before the Second World War, as a well-to-do young lady from the Hungarian middle class she had learned French from an early age (which she loved) and German soon after (which she later said she hated). She was probably also introduced to English at her grammar school. Like young ladies of her class she also travelled outside Hungary – though a brief spell in a Swiss finishing school was reportedly a disaster. This was all sharply curtailed by the Second World War, after which Hungary endured a long period of harsh repression and isolation and Mária Hári dedicated her life to serving Pető's system. There were no more foreign trips till 1968 when by happy coincidence the invitation to present her work in England coincided with the beginnings of a thaw in the closed regime of the Hungarian People's Republic.

The Wallingford window

András Pető had died the previous year, his goal of spreading his message beyond the boundaries of Hungary unfulfilled. In England Mária Hári knew there to be an agency, the Spastics Society, whose head had been approached by András Pető himself with that very goal in view and that there were people, professionals, who had visited Budapest over the previous four years and were eager to commit themselves to the task. For András Pető's newly appointed successor as Director of the Institute that he had founded this must have been not just an extraordinary and personal adventure but a mission of great professional significance.

At Castle Priory College in Wallingford, in 1968, an audience of some fifty teachers and therapists heard Mária Hári speaking not as a physician but as a pedagogue. Chapters 1 and 2 of this collection mark her thoroughgoing attempt to explicate the principles of the pedagogy at the heart of András Pető's approach for children of kindergarten and school age. Mária Hári was trying to convey the vital elements of the system to people whom she hoped and expected would then devote their resources and energy to establishing this way of working in a new land. She committed herself unreservedly to explaining what she taught student conductors in the new training course in Budapest, she threw open wide a window on to conductive pedagogy.

In 1969 Mária Hári gave a presentation in Bruges, Belgium then the next year, 1970 saw her back in Wallingford for a second invitational conference, speaking in similar vein, which provides Chapter 3 of this book. Two years later still she was at Oxford, speaking at a major international conference [5] organised by the International Cerebral Palsy Society: while little of the written record from the Oxford conference survives it appears that the window opened at Wallingford was still being held wide open. In 1975 an even larger international gathering in Dublin, again run by the International Cerebral Palsy Society, saw her devote a whole day to this task.[6]

Sometime over the later course of that decade, however, this window closed and – as all who knew her so often experienced – Mária Hári's shutters came down.

On the defensive

The papers that comprise Chapters 4 and 5 both date from 1981. The first of these was fiery, spontaneous, delivered in French, a language that Mária Hári knew and loved, perhaps reflects in its tone and content a growing realization of what had been happening over the nineteen-seventies. She had been pounding a Europe-wide conference circuit – after Oxford in 1972 she was in Olomouc, Czechoslovakia in 1973, Dublin and Denmark in 1975, Paris in 1977, Cambridge in 1979 and back in Dublin in 1981.

---

[5] Loring, A. (1972) Experts come from 25 nations for the Oxford conference. *Spastics News*, May, pp. 3,10
[6] Loring, A. (1975) Seminar experts stress major role of parents. *Spastics News*, July, pp. 3. 10

Along the way she also gave presentations in San Moreno and again in France. The dream that her Western audiences would devote their resources and energy to understanding András Pető's essentially pedagogic approach as the basis of any attempt to transplant it to new lands was not, however, turning out as she would have wished. Despite her conference appearances the day-to-day interpretation and proselytisation of Conductive Education in the West lay in other hands, outside her direct control. Her central message – that the essence of the system was conductive pedagogy, for which special pedagogic professional training was absolutely essential – went unheeded. Alternative formulations of the 'principles of Conductive Education' were proliferating in publications and in practice – and at a conference in Brussels in 1981 she publicly blew her top. The translated transcript of what she said there comprises Chapter 4.

Six months later, the paper in Chapter 5 is brief, formal and to the point. In part this may have been because it was originally presented in an unfamiliar foreign language, Russian, by a citizen of one of the Soviet Union's subject 'fraternal republics' – though as such she was delivering her message to an audience conceptually better attuned to what she was saying than were audiences in the West. In part, however, by then a new strategy for 'exporting' Conductive Education had spontaneously emerged as a Japanese organization [7] had acceded to her proposal to send people to complete the full conductor-training, under her direct personal aegis at the State Institute in Budapest. She turned her back on would-be emulators from existing professions and in 1984 began planning a second, more deliberate scheme to train foreigners at the State Institute.[8]

The nineteen eighties proved a paradoxical decade for Mária Hári. Its opening years saw her Institute under critical official examination at home then, from 1986, as if to rescue her from local criticisms, unprecedented and enthusiastic interest in its work flooded in from outside Hungary. This interest was led by families of children with cerebral palsy – but the professional interest that it brought with it was often sceptical and critical. Her unpublished

---

[7] The Warashibe Institute, Osaka
[8] The Foundation for Conductive Education, Birmingham, England

response to one critical article, which she wrote in 1990, is published in Chapter 6. By then the one-time State Institute had been 'privatised', control passing to a Board which she considered wholly commercial in its orientation and wholly contrary to the ethos that she herself held dear, to her memories of András Pető and to the ways in which she herself had directed his Institute over the years since his death.

Over the nineties and into her retirement she remained on the world stage, her presentations being now, however, what she called 'diplomatic' (by which she meant bland) as is illustrated in her so polite commentary on the Bobaths at the first world conference on neuro-developmental therapy in 1997, Chapter 7 of this book, neither struggling to explain nor fighting to defend. She remained the public face of Conductive Education, respected and revered, but no longer exercise the personal discretion and executive cutting edge that she had once so revelled in.

Towards the end of her life Mária Hári's the tone was more reflective. In her last personal conference presentation, in Chapter 8, she held steadfast to the persisting theme of the absolute necessity of proper professional preparation for conductors to secure the future of Conductive Education but she introduced and advocated a further quality: 'greater understanding of this discipline', to be achieved by extending the previous unity of practice and training to a new, treble unity – practice, training and research.

By 'research' of course she did not mean crude comparative evaluations of the sort that dogged Conductive Education across the world as it spread out of Hungary, but the broad-based, humane academic study essential to 'provide the knowledge'. She never excluded the quantifiable; indeed she had continually – and inadequately – striven to argue the achievement of Conductive Education through her own 'statistics'. But all this would now have to be left to another occasion – and to others.

Mária Hári died in October 2001.

Catching her communication

Long before the term was fashionable Mária Hári gave multi-media presentations, utilising the technology of the time. She liked to interact with her visual materials, film, sequences of still photos and overhead projections and in the privacy of the student lecture room she would readily leap on to the table, 'making the gymnastic' and using her own body to illustrate her point. She would lace her account with anecdotes and asides, and could let these lead her argument into new and unexpected turns.

None of this can one capture through the written record.

Mária Hári would draft and redraft her formal conference presentations, sometimes claiming to have scrapped everything that she had prepared back in Hungary in favour of what she had thought of on her journey over, in her hotel room the night before or even over breakfast. She took an impish pride in such claims. At times, preparation or no, she would simply extemporise. There can therefore be no single canonical version of any of her public presentations and the words presented in this book may represent any stage within the process of composition.

We present here a range of materials from carefully considered scripts which she may not actually have delivered in the present form to a transcript of a spontaneous outburst which she probably never intended written record.

Mária Hári's heritage

Over the thirty-two years represented in these pages Mária Hári was in turn authoritative and expansive, belligerent and angry, vigorous and weary – and at the end wistful and perhaps, as much as she had ever been, at peace. Over that time she created professional conductor-training and fought to hold the line. Her own chief heritage is that Conductive Education survived at all to make its own way in the modern world. But there should be more than that. For someone who thought and spoke and taught and corrected and controlled as much as she did – to the exclusion of

21

almost everything else in life – precious little remains in written form other than in the personal collections of those who knew her. A similar situation with respect of András Pető has severely impoverished the world of Conductive Education but at least Mária Hári provided a direct and authentic channel open to *his* heritage. Lack of access to *her* understandings weakens Conductive Education still more.

Today's world can be at best dubious of the very idea of special pedagogies. The conductive movement needs to marshal every possible argument to articulate conductive pedagogy and illustrate how this may be implemented to help create an education that is conductive. In the twenty-first century conductive pedagogy is being applied in contexts very, very different from the one to which Mária Hári devoted almost all her adult life. Conductors and perhaps new kinds of conductive professionals will have to refine and develop their pedagogy in a world of inclusion, choice, evidence-based practice and conflicting views of 'need' and in doing so may create Conductive Educations different in superficial form than hers. Her inspiration may prove nevertheless an indispensable tool.

This present collection offers a small contribution towards continuing Mária Hári's struggle. There probably remains little more that can be done from non-Hungarian sources to contribute primary material to help create a 'Háriology'. The onus rests squarely now upon Hungarian scholars to search personal archives for the wealth of unpublished materials that must surely survive, proper publication of which will alone ensure the critical and scholarly evaluation that her contribution to Conductive Education deserves.

.

Translation, terminology and statistics

The term 'Conductive Education' has now entered the English language and is well established in all the major British-English dictionaries – though it has still to appear in dictionaries of American English. The implications of this term have been the cause of no little confusion.

The Hungarian root word *nevel* refers to bringing up, nurturing, rearing, in other words to the process of educating and socialising children *in their entirety*. It refers to a much wider concept than simply academic education as manifest in the school curriculum, implying also the *creation, direction and correction of personal traits, behaviour, values, morals*. This is a long-established cultural concept well understood both by Hungarian people in general and the Hungarian state (and in other countries of Continental Europe too). In common parlance it is manifest in phrases such as 'he was brought up to be a soldier' or 'badly brought up' (meaning 'spoilt'). The noun *nevelés* has no commonly used equivalent in English ('upbringing' has to serve, though it strikes no immediate chord of formal processes for most English speakers). The term *konduktív nevelés* (now being abbreviated in Budapest as *KN*, perhaps by connotation with the widely used English CE) is the standard Hungarian way of referring to the system as a whole and as such was part of the official name of Mária Hári's Institute. Back in 1968 the interpreter who accompanied Mária Hári on her first visit to England used Conductive Education to translate *konduktív nevelés*, confirming an easy translation which has subsequently gained almost universal currency and is retained in this book (except in Mária Hári's Suzdal' paper, as will be explained later). It is of course essential for the conductive movement, however, that the very broad implication of this term, wider than simply academic education at school, be fully understood, both within the movement and outside.

Also essential is an understanding of the distinction between *konduktív nevelés* and *konduktív pedagógia*. This is a distinction well understood by Hungarians but less so by many English-

23

speakers amongst whom the concept of a pedagogy, a 'science and art of teaching' has dropped out of popular and professional parlance alike. As Mária Hári went to some length to insist, an education that is conductive is impossible without a conductive pedagogy. This conductive pedagogy is a 'science' in the sense that it incorporates the accumulated and formally transmitted experience and understandings of those who have gone before (as in Vygotskii's 'scientific concepts') and an 'art' in the sense that these understandings will always require transmutation through the conductor's personal empathy and imagination to rise to meet the exigencies of everyday practice. The particular characteristics of conductive pedagogy are an important theme of this book

The conductive pedagogue is called a *konduktor*. In Hungarian the person who holds the baton is a *karmester* and the word *konduktor* therefore has no association with orchestras as it does in English (though English speakers often attempt to explain Conductive Education as though it does). Nor is there an association with public transport. The only conductors in Hungarian used to be the good and bad conductors of heat, electricity etc that are used in physics. *Konduktor* as used in Conductive Education is a neutral, novel word in Hungarian, derived from the Latin *conducere,* 'to lead', to describe a professional with a particular pedagogic philosophy and style – in Mária Hári's words in Suzdal' 'a pedagogue who leads'.

The equally unfamiliar Latinism *kondukció* is anglicised here as 'conduction'. This is a common word in Hungarian within Conductive Education, referring to the linked intra-personal processes of teaching and learning that occurs between conductors and learners. Perhaps significantly, one rarely hears conduction mentioned in English other than by conductors.

A third word of little obvious meaning to most Hungarians but with a particular technical meaning within Conductive Education is *operatív*, rendered here into English as 'operative' to describe the cardinal conductive technique of 'operative observation'. The word 'operative' has little obvious meaning in English either and is therefore at risk of going unnoticed by the uninitiated reader but in this context its meaning is very specific. Here it means 'in operation', that is where conduction is in operation, where someone is being conducted and the conductor is modifying and developing the conduction according to the learner's response. It is most certainly *not* neutral observation of a learner learning but the most active possible form of interventionist, participative observation, without which there can be no conductive pedagogy.

Another item of the technical language of Conductive Education is *orthofunkció*. Anglicised as 'orthofunction' this has been widely discussed and almost as widely misunderstood. Suffice it here to indicate that it refers to an active orientation to learning on the part of learners, aware that they can and should set their own goals and, find their own ways to solve problems, and achieving satisfaction and reward in doing something new – as opposed to a *dys*functional learning cycle that teaches failure, demotivation and dependence. It does *not* mean 'walking' (this may or may not be part of orthofunctional development). Nor does it mean, for a child of school age, the same as integration or inclusion – though one may wonder what will be learnt by a child who is integrated or included and who is *not* adapting orthofunctionally.

The Hungarian word *feladatsor* has been translated in this book as 'series of tasks' or 'task series'. This does *not* mean – as may be frequently found – a prescribed series of exercises to achieve a given function, applicable to all for whom this has been decided. Rather it is what Mária Hári calls an 'algorithm' which is nothing at all to do with 'rhythm' but originally a mathematical term [9] to indicate a set of flexible procedures which if appropriately applied will resolve a mathematical problem. In common experience, think of the 'rules' that one learns in algebra to solve equations, or the simple and limited range of directions that enable one to tell someone how to find the way somewhere in a city ('first/second on the left/right, straight on...') with little need for further elaboration. Algorithms are nowadays a commonplace in writing computer software. In the context of Conductive Education task series algorithms imply a flexible, heuristic framework of activities

---

[9]   Named after the ninth century Persian mathematician, al-Kharismi

permitting a wide range of learning tasks that can and should be adapted to match the particular range of requirements of a group of learners involved as a whole and the individuals who comprise it. The particular objectives in mind and the progress that learners make in response to activities constitute a dynamic process and develop in a process of constant and carefully observed change.

Most of the manuscripts from which this book was prepared were in English, either translated from the Hungarian, for or by Mária Hári, or composed in English by herself. Two of the originals, however, were not originally in Hungarian. The French-language paper raised no particular issues of technical vocabulary but a few matters from the Russian paper merit brief note. The Russian word *vospitanie* appears directly equivalent to the Hungarian *nevelés*. In the years of the Cold War, when Soviet education was at times a matter of intense interest in the West, *vospitanie* fascinated commentators, who usually translated this Russian word into English as 'upbringing' [10]. This convention has been retained in translating Mária Hári's Suzdal' paper in order to convey some of the congruity between her own conceptual framework and wider understandings within the then Eastern Bloc – and anyway the term Conductive Education did not exist for her listeners in the same way as it would for an English-speaking audience. The Russian word *obuchenie* can be translated into English as both 'teaching' and 'learning' as it refers to a single unified interpersonal process that encompasses what in English is generally expressed and understood as a polarity. This unified teaching/learning process is comparable with conduction — though the latter perhaps implies rather more explicitly an affective (emotional) component. To stress the leading role of the pedagogue (over a more passive concept of 'a learner') *obuchenie* has been translated here as 'teaching' [11] – though do remember the implication that proper teaching in this sense also includes learning in which the learner is actively involved! Finally, in keeping with

---

[10] Bronfenbrenner, U. (1971) *Two Worlds of Childhood: USA and USSR*. London: Staples

[11].Sutton, A. (1983) An introduction to Soviet developmental psychology. *In* Meadows, S., (ed.) *Developing Thinking: approaches to children's cognitive development*. London and New York: Methuen, pp.188-205

this orientation, it is worth also remembering that in both English and Russian the words 'develop' and 'development' may have transitive as well as intransitive force. There was, however, and remains a tendency in Western thinking to favour their intransitive sense, thus 'child development' is a process in which 'a child develops...' Mária Hári's audience in Suzdal' inhabited a theoretically different world in which, at the ideological level at least, the transitive sense was favoured: social experience developed children and the task of developing children was a responsibility for all adults and for the state.

'Making the statistic'

This familiar Hári-ism referred to her Institute's established and thoroughgoing practice of compiling extensive and unfathomable numerical statements on its clients. The phrase would make those familiar with these figures despair. At first glance these descriptive statistics could impress with the sheer size of the populations involved, the span of time that they represented, and the details of age, condition, long-term outcome etc. First glance, however, provided a pitfall for the uncritical. Closer examination would lead through puzzlement to horror. The figures could represent categories for which the defining criteria were at best uncertain and at times bizarre or incomprehensible, and the more figures that one examined the less certain the picture might become. These statistics have therefore provided ready material for the critical and sceptical.

This was not a responsibility of Mária Hári's alone but the result of her Institute's inadequate understanding of the requirements of statistical collation, analysis and presentation, which continued after her retirement and her death. During her lifetime, however, she took considerable pride in this aspect of her Institute's work and in her publications and public presentations she would frequently 'make the statistic' about those who had attended her Institute, to confirm the effectiveness of Conductive Education.

Several of the papers in this collection were illustrated by statistical tables which in the lecture hall were presumably displayed by means of overhead projector and as such not always attached to the written texts. Some can be inferred from contemporary publications but in other cases these data remain lost. In either case this is indicated in the introduction to each paper.

1.

Introducing conductive pedagogy, 1968

Early in 1965 James Loring the then Director of the Spastics Society had published an article[12] previewing the work at the Society's newly built Meldreth Manor School that was to open that May. This new and pioneering school would serve children with cerebral palsy deemed ineducable under the official regulations of that time. The law in the United Kingdom, before major legislative reform in 1971, decreed that children ascertained not to be suitable for education would either remain at home in the care of their parents or be cared for by the health authorities, often in large and institutional residential settings, with no right to education. This overall situation was much as prevailed at the time in Hungary, with the exception that British society permitted a vigorous and progressive voluntary (charitable) sector of a sort altogether out of the question in the Hungarian People's Republic. In the United Kingdom independent charities were at liberty to raise funds to create innovatory services implementing alternative views of disabled children's capabilities.

The Spastics Society's Meldreth Manor School had been planned to be just such a mould-breaking innovation. It would still be residential (on a 'family home' basis) but develop its own 'social education' syllabus to create levels of independence acceptable at home, in a centre or elsewhere, stimulate emotional development, self-help and communication, and provide 'such general education as the child can absorb', all this within a regime that would emphasise the importance of play.

In Hungary this article came to the attention of András Pető, by now a sick man near the end of his life and much concerned to hand on the torch of the system that he had developed. Much impressed by what he understood to be planned at Meldreth Manor

---

[12] Loring, J. (1965) Meldreth: a pioneer unit for the training of spastic children, *Special Education*, 55, (1), 20-24

he wrote to James Loring, the man ultimately responsible for this bold innovation, proposing that the Director of the Spastics Society should help establish Pető's work safely outside Hungary. A correspondence ensued but in September 1967 Pető died. It was only in June of the following year that James Loring, accompanied by his wife Anita, travelled to Budapest to see for himself the work at Pető's State Institute.

The Lorings were very impressed with what they saw and invited Mária Hári to make a reciprocal visit to describe first-hand the work for which she was now responsible. This was coincidentally a time of significant liberalisation in the Hungarian People's Republic (relative to what had gone before) and Mária Hári's visit was organised surprisingly quickly, occurring in October of the same year.[13]

Mária Hári came from Hungary with an interpreter and the first paper, presented here, was read for her by Ester Cotton. Things at first went very slowly. Questions, delivered and answered through the translator, also went very slowly. By lunchtime, however, Mária Hári was responding to questions directly, with less and less recourse to the interpreter, and communication speeded up. She told that she had brought the interpreter only because her English teacher in Hungary had said that nobody in England would be able to understand her English. Her presentation was illustrated and enlivened by films of various groups within the Institute.

The formal, slightly stilted language of the original manuscript bears the marks of having been written by an accomplished speaker of the sort of English common to educated Hungarians who have studied the language in Hungary. This original is presumably the interpreter's carefully prepared text based upon a Hungarian original in which Mária Hári was able to express herself with natural ease and fluency. Though in preparing the text for this publication a few words and items of punctuation have been changed to a more English usage, in one sense this text may be counted as Mária Hári's authentic voice.

---

[13] Knowles, J. W. (1968) The Peto method is more than a transitory idea. *Spastics News*, December, p.7

The paper does, however, maintain one Hári-ism of the type that persisted endearingly in her English speech for the rest of her life: 'the contact' (which she always pronounced with the stress on its second syllable). Because of this, for a whole generation who learned of Conductive Education in English in Budapest, 'the contact' became and has remained one of the technical terms of the conductive field in the English-speaking world. This familiar translation has been retained here. The original Hungarian word *kapczolat* means 'link' or 'connection' and can also be used to refer to the fastening of a garment. Perhaps a better translation in this context would have been 'bond', with all its psychological associations. Be that as it may, this vital, affective, interpersonal aspect of conductive pedagogy was not in the event taken up explicitly by contemporary attempts to establish conductive practices in the United Kingdom – even though, in the same year as Mária Hári's first appearance at Wallingford, the first American visitor to her Institute in Budapest, James House, had immediately recognised this factor at work and put it at the forefront of his published report.[14] He called it 'love'.

This event was held at Castle Priory, the Spastics Society's staff-training college, and mainly involved people, within the Society and without, concerned to set up something along Pető's lines in this country. The latter included Ester Cotton, Margaret Parnwell [15] and Margaret Ram. They too showed films of their work.

---

[14] House, J. (1968) Breakthrough in Budapest; an interview. *Ideas of Today*, 16(3), pp.110-114.
[15] Cotton, E., Parnwell, M. (1968) Conductive Education with special reference to severe athetoids in a non-residential setting. *Journal of Mental Subnormality*, 14(1), pp50-56.

Address given by Dr Hári of the Institute for Conductive Education of the Motor Disabled, Budapest

Paper read at a study day, Castle Priory College, Wallingford, 12 October 1968

Dear Friends,

I was very pleased to accept your kind invitation to give an account of Pető's Conductive Education. The active work carried out to educate and rehabilitate cerebrally palsied children can be considered one of England's greatest traditions. We consider it a great pleasure that England was the first beside Hungary to employ Conductive Education to tackle the above-mentioned problems.

I believe it impossible to acquaint you fully with Conductive Education within the available time, either in a lecture or by film. Trusting in your understanding I shall give a brief account on the work of our Institute and the most important fundamental principles and practices of our work. I shall give some organisational information and a few details on our results. I choose this form because in my opinion discussion after the lecture will be more dynamic and this way of imparting knowledge is in accordance with the conductive principles to which you can devote your attention and time more economically. In the spirit of these thoughts permit me to enter upon my subject.

First of all, the education, teaching and medical treatment of children suffering from cerebro- and spino-motoric dysfunction is different in every country but at the same time it is uniformly agreed that educational work, the management of severely impaired children, their treatment and provision, should be carried out by specialists who do their work isolated from one another.

The Conductive Education system differs from all other systems mainly in that the rehabilitation, treatment and educational work for cerebrally palsied children are a homogeneous inseparable unity.

It is assumed that except for most severe cases the impaired nervous system possesses a residual capacity which under optimal conditions can be mobilised and renders rearrangement of the uncoordinated functional unit possible. On the basis of the results obtained from Professor Pető's work between 1945 and 1963, the Hungarian government provides for Conductive Education of children with cerebro- and spino-motoric dysfunction, also for the training of experts, the conductors, at a high level at the Hungarian State Institute for Conductive Education of the Motor Disabled and Conductors' College. According to the government's decision the problem of children suffering with central nervous system diseases – besides being an economic, social and medical problem – *is considered above all as a pedagogic problem.*

In Hungary education is an *integrated state affair.* The education of cerebro-spino-motoric dysfunctional children is also within this system, as is the building up of a network belonging to the central Institute.

The work of the Institute consists of four inter-related tasks:

> Conductive Education – as rehabilitation;

> conductor-training;

> scientific research work;

> keeping records and following up each patient.

Admission to our Institute is preceded by a 'conductive examination'. The criterion for Conductive Education is whether there is a possibility in any way to create contact with the children. We have groups of twelve to twenty-four children. We put children of different age, sex and capability levels *in groups with a view to education.* Within these educative units the principles of

34

conductive pedagogy prevail. One of these principles is to develop the children's emotional equilibrium and create a positive atmosphere by, among other things, satisfying the demand of a community.

Group activity facilitates speech and movement. The mere presence of a companion induces positive emotions in the child. This plays a great role in increasing the effectiveness of function. A child living with his family gets support from his parents but hardly any task, while within the group the whole group is given assignments and the child is forced to be independent because he sees no one nearby from whom he could immediately and permanently obtain help. The conductor is not simply and only beside him, she is *with the whole group.* In collective work the child is given examples by which he sees that the task *can be* accomplished and tries to imitate because he wants to carry on with the group. He even tries to carry out things that he would not try to do if he were in the focus of attention – owing to a lack of self-assurance – or, if he did, his effort would be exaggerated and this always means increased rigidity. A further advantage of collective work is that the children within the group must copy each other within certain forms.

At the same time conductive pedagogy renders *individual care and relationships within the group possible.* The conductor directs the community and builds up the conditions of activity. She always takes care to hold the children's attention and maintain a cheerful atmosphere, which offers the possibility of getting close to the individual. The group is broken down in smaller units that solve the given tasks in a similar fashion but besides this everyone has his own personal way of solving the task, which is laid down in the programme too, and is held responsible for carrying out that task. The sense of their own importance in the collective work also develops in the children.

The conductor is acquainted with all the children's capacity for performance, watches their development and modifies individuals' programmes accordingly. *The pre-condition of Conductive Education is continuous experimental observation concentrated in one person*, the appointed conductor. Conductive observation extends to physiological processes and movements and, further, to every minute and manifestation of the cerebral-palsied child. What is more, conductive observation takes place during operative Conductive Educational work. We may therefore assert that this method is absolutely different from the mere conventional registration of clinical examination.

Conductive pedagogy naturally applies individual and social-psychological rules too. For example, the conductor pretends not to notice the child while he is performing his task because focusing attention upon him would make it much more difficult for the child. On the other hand, she intervenes immediately if she sees that the child is not satisfied with his own performance. In such cases she helps the child to success with the aid of facilitations. One of her main tasks is to provide the child with experience of success. Facilitation is a device that eventually helps the child to carry out the task independently with less and less aid. Conductive facilitation abolishes itself. The road to functional capacity leads through *a series of tasks*. The series of tasks is a carefully selected and built algorithmic construction, in which if analysed all postures can be found, from the lying to the standing position, as well as all kinds of movements, gross and fine too.

I should like to mention one or two examples of the task series, and by doing so refer to their characteristics. For example, one of the task series in the lying position for contract athetoids leads every one of them to grasp in all positions, to turn prone and supine and reverse, to sit up and relax themselves to the extent of being able to lift their arms high and then put them down again to their sides. The result of this task series is to achieve lifting of the arms to head level.

This final aim is broken down into parts. At first the children, while turning on their sides stretch their arms to shoulder level. When they have achieved this position, they turn on to their backs, keeping their arms in position. Thus they are lying on their backs, holding their stretched arms up vertically, then they roll over on to their sides and stomachs but now the arms are stretched beside the head. Finally, they turn back, keeping their arms beside their heads. Eventually they can stretch their arms high in a sitting position beside the head and lie down on their backs. When the aim is achieved without transitional tasks, these can be left out. Thus the series become shorter and shorter.

Some of the elements in the task series are repeated in different situations. For example, sitting up and lying down with a stick in the hand is followed by letting the stick go and raising the arms with open hands. After repeated sitting up and lying down with a stick in the hand comes turning sideways and backwards with a stick in the hand. Then further sitting up and lying down follow so that the child's head is where his feet were previously. Finally rolling over on to the side and prone position, then sitting up and lying down again complete the series, but in such a way as *prescribed by us as the final goal.*

It is fascinating for the children to accomplish the different elements of the series, and *as every partial result prepares the success of the following one, success becomes always greater.* As a result the positive satisfaction of the child's emotions increases more and more. His interest towards the tasks and the intensity of participation increases crescendo-like to the last task, which is at the same time evidence of the concrete result attained by the child through the series.

Contradictory elements of movement follow one another: sitting up, lying down, grasping and letting go, turning sideways and reverse, taking the stick above the head, placing it on the stomach, lifting the foot up and down on the plinth, tightening and relaxing and so on. By these means the whole exercise series becomes more harmonious.

The series of tasks contain many elements that are not in close connection with movement. The children sing or speak while moving. This is of great importance for the athetoids who cannot speak (apart, up, down, over, out, in, etc.); possibly monosyllables in a form that can be expected from them should accompany their movements. When moving, they become familiar with the concepts of space and time (because their task is defined within these limits) and their laterality of disturbances are also eliminated. It happens many times that they also observe, imitate and criticise their own and their friends' work and often offer them help.

The co-ordination of successive movements, their arrangement in time and the automatic joining of respective elements are strengthened by the rhythm produced by speech. The perception of rhythm and motion are strictly connected: as rhythm binds the elements of motion it promotes conscious control.

It is characteristic of task series that they do not consist of therapeutic movements but details which promote conscious functional possibilities. The choreo-athetoid child for example does not do hand movements but learns to move his whole body by command of the cortex. Thus we understand that the floor exercises pave the way for writing, namely the children learn to rise and to sit down, hold their head, hold the pencil, co-ordinate their extremities and if necessary not move them. That is all that is necessary for writing by hand.

The tasks motivated by the conductor always cause pleasure and invoke attention, and the result is the child's increasingly independent work. We make the exercises colourful and varied and in addition to the tasks we also assign activities that provide pleasurable experiences. These experiences stimulate expression and bring about positive preparedness for solving current tasks and expanding knowledge. These *interpolated* activities are not only a relaxation which spontaneously interrupts the seemingly rigorous exercises but an active experience of the day's work programme that is characteristic of Conductive Education, and a deliberate and programme-like method for conveying knowledge.

We consider the task series as instruments and methods to develop the child's efficiency and willingness to act, which is the precondition of obtaining any kind of knowledge. At the same time, it is made possible for the conductor to transmit the curriculum and for the child to absorb information. It should therefore be clear why we do not separate the series of exercises from the 'transmitting-acquiring' process of education. This is one of the most important basic principles of Conductive Education.

Should I mention one further feature it would be the following. If we examine any other method or system we see that in almost every case even the members of the best co-operating team, using uniform principles, deal separately with each phase, one after the other, always keeping specific aims in mind, whereas in the conductive system the various particular principles are combined and take place simultaneously.

In accomplishing any task, just like when acquiring any other function, conscious awareness is the most important factor. It is therefore imperative that the child should understand the task and be willing to carry it out. The child does not always find the way of doing something, he must be conducted. With the aid of applied inductive facilitations sometimes we obtain the result in a round-about way. On the other hand, after experience of successful movement, we make children aware of the activity that they have accomplished. This means that if the child has carried out the task in some way, perhaps with the help of applied facilitations, we identify the result as a realised task solution. We make the child realise immediately exactly what he has done by relating it to the second signalling system, speech. The child also becomes familiar with his movements by learning to express what he is doing in words too. Children are always aware of the starting point and result when carrying out a task. Inductive facilitation offers an opportunity for activisation, moreover it gives the child the possibility of feeling that he has discovered the solution by himself. By this method his inclination for solving tasks develops.

Let us now turn to another aspect of conductive observation. Conductive observation serves the following purpose: the conductor can give supplementary information when the child's own reafferents are not sufficient. The conductor keeps in mind the individual way of carrying out a task and before the next occasion she reminds the child of the right way of doing it. When repeating the tasks she decreases the facilitations until the task tied to the intention is carried out successfully, without facilitation. A task connected with speech becomes conscious in every detail. The stability of speech is higher than that of the movement series, therefore the stability of joining the parts of the movement is ensured by the *directive effect of speech.*

Parts of the activity series join closely together only if we repeat the developed movement series within the most different functions during the day. By such repetition the stereotypes take root in the same way as knowledge becomes positive by its use. *The condition to automatise the movement series* is to repeat the established movement series during the day within more complex tasks. Here we arrive at another very important factor in Conductive Education, the daily *programme.* This differs from all other daily timetables in that the readiness and habits of behaviour established during the so called 'important' periods are used and further developed deliberately in a programmatic fashion during the break which is generally regarded as lost time. Thus the special functions are developed unperceived by the children, but permanently and continually. Within the daily programme *the readiness of behaviour and the development of habits* are realised by the conductor, ensuring in one person the steady and identical application of stereotypes and continuity. As the conductor can utilise every part of the day in many respects, all day long she makes the children practise the basic abilities necessary for acquiring knowledge of writing and speaking.

As a matter of fact the material of curriculum subjects does not remain within the sphere of school activity but also develops during the break, in the seemingly unproductive period, through the very process of observation. Thus *the daily timetable is nothing else but a deliberate, purposeful conveyance of knowledge distributed through the day,* which has an effect on the whole group and the individual alike in every hour and minute of the day. This renders possible the rational utilization of time. The daily programme is formulated by the conductor's observation. The advantage of Conductive Education is that the child is not bound to one person but to the conductor system: within this system the conductors are equal to each other but at the same time completely informed and able to direct the development of a child and everything concerning his education.

The conductor teaches the child to hold and use a pencil, to carry out the necessary finger movements, to fix the paper, to hold his torso, to follow hand movements with his eyes, to keep the feet on the floor as well as obtain the knowledge of stereoscopic ideas, conception of shape, to write, speak, sing, play and to learn music. She is able to follow and help the child's active learning process all day long, the development and refining of his intellectual function, observational capacity and resourcefulness.

The close relationship between conductor and children enables her to fulfill their desire for play and joy. The conductors do not take into consideration crying as a means of communication within the group (anyway, this manifestation of feelings is most rare in the Institute). But on the contrary she pays great attention to the smallest movement or change of mimicry because this may indicate that the child's self-respect has suffered because he did not attain the expected results. In such a case, instead of offering psycho-pedagogically harmful consolation and affection, she displays a friendly attitude and helps the child to overcome his difficulties.

Thus the training of an expert in accordance with the demands of conductive pedagogy is an important condition for successful work. The training of specialists for this special task takes place in the Institute during a four-year programme of active work. The efficiency of a conductor will be demonstrated by her work during the active course. The training is constant and the Institute has the possibility to make a thorough choice of those who are suitable for this vocation. So far, twenty conductors have qualified and at present an additional sixty-eight are studying.

We have carefully followed up the development of 866 individuals who have spent more than one month at our Institute. On the basis of the evaluations we tried to determine how many of our patients could adapt themselves to social life after leaving the Institute. The aim of Conductive Education is to terminate dysfunctions in order to enable the patients of our Institute to attend normal general, then middle schools and technical schools respectively after leaving, instead of a special school. The efficiency of Conductive Education was studied as to its results by a computer

41

analysis as follows: during the check-up we determined *how many of the patients 'became fit for study and work respectively',* how many *became independent* and what percentage of the patients were unable to become self-supporting.

72.28% of the patients were cerebral-palsied, 13.70% paraplegic, and 9.12% hemiplegic; according to diagnoses, 75.18% of the patients are children, 24.82% adults. Before admission it was generally believed that the children are incapable of learning, therefore after admission nearly all begin their studies in the first class.

I shall conclude my lecture by giving a brief account of some apparent characteristics.

> First of all, I mention that conductive observation is continuous. This is not cross sectional but determines functions and their adequate possible changes.

> Screening for admission is based on the possibility of integration within the group and not on the severity of dysfunction.

> The above criterion concerns admission of those who become residents because to achieve beneficial results, constant change of environment, change in the morning and at night, difference between treatment at night and in the day, cannot be permitted. The object of Conductive Education is not to accommodate severely dysfunctional patients in an Institute or to send them to a special school but to accomplish a basic task, to render a normal education possible, travelling in the streets, self-support and work.

> In order to bring about equilibrium between child and environment, we do not change the environment, but adapt the child's constitution.

> In the conductive system, teaching of movements,

treatment, education and care do not take place separately in time and space but in a homogenous unity and at the same time.

The teaching of movement, the development of the second signalling system and its utilization are applied in a dialectic inter-relation.

The usual college instruction system is not suitable here, even temporary training in the field of practice. Training of conductors can be solved only within the sphere of practical work.

The picture given here of Conductive Education cannot be complete but in the forthcoming discussion I think we can clear up all the problems.

2.

A psycho-pedagogy, 1968

Mária Hári's second paper from that first Wallingford conference is less discursive, more analytical than the first. Again the original bears the marks of a professional Hungarian translator and it looks like considerable care was taken in its preparation. The text is 'dense', probably far too much so for oral presentation of new ideas and practices to an audience unfamiliar with what is being discussed or its conceptual context.

Her theoretical presentation of fundamental principles extends out from the pedagogic into the psychological and bears signs of the dominant intellectual tradition in her country at that time,[16] presenting conductive pedagogy as a new social quality, dependent upon cortical function (she could have added *specifically human* cortical function), invoking the second signalling system of reality, speech, to link the conscious and the motoric. And behind all this stands the group, the community, the nested system of collectives within the Institute as the basis for satisfactory development of individuality and personality. [17]

Mária Hári's two carefully prepared formal presentations to the Wallingford conference in 1968 together comprise her most comprehensive and coherent account of Conductive Education, conductive pedagogy and their theoretical underpinnings yet identified.

---

[16] English-language readers will find an authoritative contemporary collection of papers illustrating that tradition in Cole, M. and I. Maltzman, I.,(ed.) (1969) *A handbook of contemporary Soviet psychology*, New York, Basic Books.

[17] Bronfenbrenner, U. (1971) *Two worlds of childhood: U.S. and U.S.S.R.,* London: George Allen and Unwin, especially pages 49-51.

Fundamental principles of conductive pedagogy

Paper read at a study day, Castle Priory College, Wallingford, 12 October 1968

In the Conductive Education process various effects create a dialectic unity. The sum of these components offers something qualitatively new, not an integrity consisting of parts but a qualitatively new compound with peculiar characteristics and effects whose catalyst is nothing else but the social view.

Movement as a 'task'

In movement, according to the traditional opinion, the motor function of the muscles is of critical importance. The latest concept, however, regards perception and movement as a unified sensori-motor function organised by subcortical structures. The new so-called neurophysiological, global methods therefore employ reflexively associated global movement instead of single-purpose movement of the muscles.

Thus conductive pedagogy relies upon organisation of movement at a higher level of integration. According to relevant experiences, motor learning making use of cortical functions, or even under their control, is much more efficient and faster than mechanical practice. The child is expected to understand the task and to wish success, instead of mechanically repeating certain predetermined elements of movement.

Guidance through a task series

Within the unity of Conductive Education development of correct activity follows an articulated (algorithmic) programme. The sequence of superimposed part-problems leads each participant member of the group to solutions to the target functions set. The part-objectives are gradually omitted with time, the task series is reduced, implementation of the activity becomes increasingly economical and new objectives may be specified.

The integrity of duties determined within the task series involves each part of the organism, even those functioning inadequately in the operation of the body scheme. The solution type of each different task ensures replacement of the dysfunctional form of organisation on the part of the nervous system, overlaying each function with an orthofunctional, integrated form.

Creating the experience of movement

Solving a deliberately set problem may sometimes fail without our assistance. The conductor (the qualified Conductive Education instructor) will increase the individual's spontaneous activity by promoting the patient's discovery of how to arrive at a solution, by setting appreciable and controllable objectives and guiding the tasks. The experience of movement thus brought about, which is the basis of the first signal system, is connected by the conductor to the second signal system, speech, and thereby made immediately conscious as an actually realised solution to the problem. This in turn makes all the details of the activity similarly conscious. The associated speech transfers the entire function to the level of an intellectual operation. Mental determination of the task (the intention) and the specification of the rhythm facilitate rational in-time co-ordination, which is the connection of the individual elements of the movement process. Determination of an objective means preparation in advance. Preliminary determination of a given function through speech enables the individual under training to arrive at the solution in a much shorter way instead of by trial and error. With rhythm and movement elements engaged the method promotes conscious control of movement itself; stability of speech exceeds that of the movement sequence, and therefore connection of the details of the movement is ensured by the child's own speech. The relationship between the objective and the road leading to it is understood by the pupil and the method employed to achieve the target will exert permanent effect and grow into an experience adoptable at any time.

The programme

The integrated forms used for solution of the task problems go beyond the closed framework of the task sequences and will be repeated in each field of the daily programme. The skill developed during these repetitions will be the result of dynamic rather than mechanical imprint. Each activity on the programme may take from ten to ninety minutes. The curriculum is realised within the framework of studies, assuming the form of daily and/or weekly timetables in which the transition times are similarly important. Only at very first glance does the programme of the Institute appear to be of a character in which every activity specified by the curriculum, such as various studies, would differ from each other. If looked at more thoroughly each study will be found to consist of a number of similar elements. The same techniques, for standing up, speech, manual and other practices, or their application, will be seen in many apparently different activities. Thus the isolated parts of the programme will be transformed into an uninterrupted process. This continuity will in turn make the activity thus developed useful, the orthofunction gradually habitual. The programme of Conductive Education is characterised by maximum concentration. Each learning activity affects the field of the next one and both exert interactions. The ability to solve problems is similarly overlapping. Thus each part of the programme represents receipt of conscious information and at the same time practice of some functions already developed.

Personality in the community

The multilateral activity offered by the programme serves the development of personality. The activities deliberately learned through each event of the daily programme become habitual and the habits thus developed will soon grow conscious, as if built into the personality.

A fundamentally new feature of the education of patients with locomotor disorders is utilization of the relationship between humans and their social environment, due to their inseparable unity. Education and the formation of character are appropriate tools out of which the favourable habits of community life, the attraction towards community, are then developed. Under community conditions those suffering from dysfunctions learn to live and act deliberately. A well-organised community will promote any stimulated, controlled active-learning process and therefore represents an essential factor in increasing the educational effect. While individual treatment is emphasised in the rehabilitation of those suffering from dysfunctions all over the world, the development of community co-operation is one of the most important conductive duties.

The groups create communities within the Institute. In this work conductors and patients, children and adults, as well as all the other employees of the Institute, exert close co-operation. The occasional integration of the individual collectives (including outpatients) in the form of common work, games, film projections, meals etc. promotes their creation of a large but closely related community, even though the age, sex or condition of the members differ. The patients of the individual groups feel such a close relationship with their companions and conductors that they maintain this relationship with each other and the Institute even after they have left, and frequently return for a visit.

Children grow emotionally well balanced in the Institute and of a positive basic mood in which satisfaction of their community requirements is a major influence. In the collectives thus developed, the mere presence of others will give rise to positive emotions in the children and these dispositional tensions are of the utmost importance in increasing their capabilities.

The results achieved and demonstrated in the course of the educational process affect the entire group and enhance the activity of the other members. In teamwork the individuals witness actual examples showing that the objectives can be accomplished. The traditions of the group are of almost compulsory effect. The experience of success is of similarly great importance within the community. Social acknowledgment is a motivating factor of nearly indispensable force. In a community patients successfully attempt to solve task problems which they would never dare tackle alone because of lack of self-confidence; if they alone were the focus of attention, their efforts would increase to a detrimental excitement. The conductor is with the entire group and not only the lone individual. In solving a given task problem the individual is compelled to act independently as there is nobody to render immediate assistance or to be relied upon with exclusive rights. Thus the group will increase self-assurance, reduce anxiety, augment willpower and relieve the patients from their existing complexes regardless of age.

Our groups include children of different diagnoses, dysfunctions, age and sex, making an unhomogeneous impression. Their members however exhibit identical part-dysfunctions, in endeavour, emotions, abilities and similar interests. These are characteristics of the most significant importance in our categorisation. The groups are sub-divided into similar units whose members solve given tasks problems similarly. Within these units, however, individual members have their own individual methods to solve problems as specified by the programme. The conductor controls the solution, modifies the personal programme to correspond to improvement of the output level and restricts allowances accordingly until the function is performed in the shortest, most regular and efficient manner.

The results of Conductive Education

In determining learning ability the method employed by the Institute differs from generally usual examination techniques. Admission is decided upon the possibility of creating the contact with the child that is the pre-condition of fitting into a group. To achieve successful results the child is often prepared within the activity of the School for Parents, with the patient's parents fully co-operating in such cases. Through conductive pedagogy children suffering from dysfunctions and previously believed unable to learn may also be educated. Depending on their condition the children thus admitted spend a shorter or longer period of time in the Institute. According to our follow-up examinations the average period spent in the Institute is from ten to twenty-four months, during which the children become independent and are prepared for school or work. Assessment of results is made possible by description of functions through numerical evaluation. Thus abilities assessed at admission and on leaving can be compared. This measurement method, however, does not indicate the extend of rigidity or reduction of over-movement in a precise manner and cannot be applied to show the complex structural changes of the nervous system – but may still be considered as sufficiently objective. The actual results, however, are indicated by how far the locomotor-disordered patient is able to enter productive society and not by the above indices.

Of the 364 who left the Institute[18] in 1968 a total of 36.32% left in a recovered condition while 13.18% remained as they entered. Furthermore, 34.9% of the former group now attend primary schools, 4.13% are working, the majority of the remainder being of kindergarten age.

Through gradual but continuous development over the last twenty years and with all the relevant data and experience collected we are now in the position to sum up and present the results achieved by follow-up examination of those who left earlier. The observations cover a period of about ten to fifteen years. The life of a total of 1,000 former patients was followed after completion of training in the Institute. The follow-up of these individuals was started with the precise purpose of collecting information on the results possible through conductive pedagogy, as well as on their duration, and of finding out whether our patients have actually grown independent, how their studies in school have progressed and how they work. Statistical processing of the follow-up data was performed in the University Computer Centre under the direction of Miklós Hámori, senior scientific associate and with the co-operation of Pál Hidegh from our Institute.

---

[18] The tables to which she is referring are missing

A total of 866 from the 1,000 former patients selected at random between 1 January and 1 August 1968 have reported upon invitation to the follow-up examination. The average index showing conditions upon admission, leaving and follow-up (which presents the sum of the scores as a percentage of the maximum possible score figure) reveals that the patients who left have maintained the degree of achieved function over ten to fifteen years after leaving.

Simultaneous to the introduction of Conductive Education for patients with locomotor disorders in Hungary, the education and training of conductors was also commenced in our Institute – at a higher-education level in combination with practical conductive activity. This continuous conductor-training ensures the personnel base for the recovery of locomotor-disorder patients. To facilitate the correct design of conductor-training a national survey of demand is in progress.

The activity of our Institute and the results of our conductive method have already attracted much interest in a number of countries. Conductive Education represents a new field in pedagogy. Exploration of its rules relies on several scientific disciplines, involving all of them, however, at the same time.

3.

The great and the good, 1970

In 1970 the Lorings visited Budapest again, observing and considering the work of Mária Hári's State Institute in detail. James Loring came back convinced that we should reconsider our whole approach to the teaching of young disabled children and publicly posed three challenging questions: have we become too complacent; do we devote too much time to individual tuition and are we failing to treat the child as a whole being from an educational point of view?[19] In the October of that year Mária Hári found herself back in Wallingford, at a rather different meeting from that of two years previously.

It was the sort of meeting that she always professed herself to hate but which she in fact always did rather well, the chance to address and mingle with 'eminent experts'. These included head-teachers of the Spastics Society's schools, senior members of its administrative and advisory staff and influential figures from special education, paediatrics and the Department of Education and Science. A brief published report [20] included photographs that suggest a cheery social occasion with Mária Hári tinkling the tea-cups with the best of them.

Despite this paper's title only its opening paragraphs related to the history of Conductive Education. This briefly dispatched, Mária Hári proceeded to expatiate on the work itself.

The original text for this paper differs from those for her two presentations made at the same venue two years previously. Those had been carefully formulated presentations, precisely expressed in

---

[19] Loring, J. (1970) Three important questions we must answer on child training. *Spastics News*, September, p.2

[20] Anon (1970) Experts confer on Peto work, *Spastics News*, November , p. 5

elaborate English prose. This is quite different, with short sentences, some laboriously stated, asides and parentheses, questions to herself and no clear line of argument. The actual typewritten manuscript is heavily corrected, overwritten in her own hand, and looks to be intended as notes for speaking rather than as a formal text to be read aloud.

In contrast to the earlier papers, this one appears to have been written in English by Mária Hári herself – it certainly 'sounds like' how she spoke in English. If she did receive help in this it was probably not from the same interpreter involved two years earlier, thus the word 'connection' is used here where elsewhere she would have said 'contact'.

We know from the published report that she also showed films of children's progress but not what else she did or said there. The paper presented here may well have been accompanied by other, more nitty-gritty pedagogic exposition, such as she had given to her audience of teachers and therapists at Wallingford two years before. As it stands, however, it could be read – and heard – as reassuringly congruent with ideas already in the professional domain in the United Kingdom at the time. Be that as it may, nothing seems subsequently to have happened to suggest that this fairly high-ranking professional audience, 'mainly people who would be asked to advise parents and therapists, or who [were] responsible for medical and educational services', went away converted to new ways of thinking or acting.

The short story of Conductive Education

Paper presented to a two-day conference, Castle Priory College, Wallingford, October 1970

Professor Pető was the founder – he was very resolute and uncompromising. In Austria he was director of several sanitoria (he worked in the fields of neurology, psychiatry, tuberculosis, psychotherapy, biochemistry and was also a publisher and editor of a bulletin) before he returned to Budapest in 1938, and in 1945 he was called upon to teach 'movement therapy' at the College of Special Education. This was when I first met him. He was given two empty rooms and thirteen so-called uneducable children from a home and began work with the help of four medical students. The number of patients grew and the little institute maintained its own out-patients' service. After a two-year trial period without a budget, the results were examined by a group of paediatricians and it was found that some of the children had become independent and the others were able to attend normal schools. Only after consideration of this fact did the institution become a *state institution*, get a budget and in 1952 move to the present building.

After this there still followed a trial period of more than ten years, as it was not understood why Professor Pető stuck consistently to his original ideas, and the struggle for acceptance of Conductive Education and the concept of a conductor became a very long one. From 1952 until 1963 the Institute belonged to the Health Ministry, to the part where the uneducable children belonged. Only after a period of almost eighteen years was Conductive Education adopted as an educational system and in 1963 a state decree was issued. This declared that:

> the education of people disabled by damage to the central nervous system at all stages of their lives – nursery school and pre-training for work – all neuromotoric dysfunctions, was the task of the Institute;

the training of conductors was to be undertaken at the Institute (and has been established since 1965);

the Institute was to build up a network across the country;

scientific research was to be carried out.

The conductor-training course is a higher-education course of four years. The curriculum of conductor education is the same as that of teacher-education but includes special knowledge and the relationship between all dysfunctions. The training includes experience gained in real practical work along with a sense and the fact of responsibility, supervised, criticised and co-related by senior conductors, alongside the theoretical studies. After successfully passing the state examination at the end of the eighth semester the student-conductor receives a conductor qualification.

After telling the short story of its development I would like to introduce Conductive Education itself, starting with a description of the groups. We have in the Institute 200 resident and 250 ambulant (ambulant means something like out-patients) and it depends on the handicap whether somebody has to come three times a week or once a month. In respect of differentiation, it is possible out of 200 residents to make fourteen groups and many sub-groups, to build approximately homogeneous communities out of them. Still, the seemingly most homogeneous communities are diverse and types of dysfunction are also generally mixed and the forms pass one into the other. (They work eventually at different levels, in different ways).

In Tables 1-3 [21] I show the distribution of residents according to the clinical type, age, school age and diagnosis. As one can see the distribution by no means follows the clinical diagnosis, as educational requirements may be decisive in this and at certain times of the day the distribution is different. They are all different in respect of hearing, vision speech and movement capabilities.

---

[21] These tables were not attached to the manuscript but are probably similar to Tables 1-3 in M. Hari and K. Akos (1988) *Conductive Education*. London: Routledge, pp.1-2 which was published in its original Hungarian edition in 1971.

Among our children some:

> are suspected of being deaf;
>
> have hearing difficulties;
>
> have supranuclear muscular imbalance;
>
> have squints;
>
> have refractive errors;
>
> have retinal disease;
>
> do not speak at all;
>
> their speech is unintelligible;
>
> their speech is understandable but dysarthric;
>
> 45% of the residents cannot stand without support.

Athetoid children have to learn everything – to listen, to look, to follow a moving object, to understand, to make their wishes and needs known, to discriminate, to control and co-ordinate their bodies and to acquire skills. It is not surprising that teaching them needs special skills. The curriculum is extensive and they are slow, so it is necessary for them to have more time from the teacher. If the children are not given the chance to learn the skills that they need to achieve at school then the teaching is hindered and, if they are not given the chance to learn *how to co-ordinate,* self-care and other functions are also hindered. But if the children are conducted gradually and purposefully, building on the smallest actions, they can learn to build on their skills. This is the background for redefining the teaching of function to these children.

Conductive does not mean a special technique but that teaching is concerned all the time with guiding, it is a pedagogy. Every child has to create his own appropriate technique for solving his problems and this is guided by the conductor.

According to our principles we teach children to cope with the circumstances, we endeavour to support them to be continuously engaged in some activity, like normal children, and to develop in them the capacity to initiate. Our experience helps us plan our work in the group and for the group to meet emotional and social needs.

Conductive Education meets the same requirements as normal education and the pedagogical principles are the same, but these requirements are complicated by the requirement of simultaneously learning elementary functions which cannot be developed spontaneously without teaching as in normal children. Similarly to the scheme of requirements in which the tuition plan is broken down, these further requirements are also summarised and the programme stipulates achievements which can be measured exactly. These later serve the purpose of acquiring and applying subject matter of tuition.

This unified programme is determined naturally, by the level of the development of those participating. By gradually increasing the level and its requirements, the content and characteristics of their work, dependency and self-responsibility show an ever-changing picture and, in accordance with this, the entire daily programme alters. This is how the programme is determined by the level of development. In the introductory period (after admission) the main purpose is to *adapt the child to the group* on the basis of his individual capabilities, *using observation.* The child can be switched over, but only gradually, to the new daily programme (to do so-called 'work') and to take responsibility for himself. This can take six to seven days or up to two to three months. In the subsequent work building of a good *connection* is of greatest importance, both between the child and other children and between the child and the conductors who get to know the child. From the beginning gradual decrease of dysfunctional practices, their change and the building of new *habits,* are made constantly step by step. The child is examined by a paediatrician, neurologist, orthopedist, audiologist, neuro-opthalmologist, dentist etc., who make suggestions regarding the child's needs. Thus a basic picture of the child is drawn using these along with our observations and the next aims to be achieved are recorded.

The requirements regarding sitting, taking meals, the way of self-transport are worked out in accordance with current abilities and adequate demands made for *fulfilling* every task are laid down and kept as evidence connected with the daily programme. Multilateral requirements are set for all kinds of lessons with details of the proposed time to achieve them. All the functions required for taking part in the lessons of the day are performed one way or another from the very start of the day, with maximum support at the beginning. During the course of the voluntary learning process the *requirements gradually grow* in relation to the slow improvements in functioning. Qualitative alterations (differentiation of basic solutions) may last hardly a moment at first and be closely connected to definite conditions. Repeating these new skills in a variety of given occasions means that they become established and can be used in a variety of conditions and circumstances. The child's daily programme alters corresponding to the qualitative increase of independence up until he leaves the Institute. Before discharge we create outside circumstances and try to give experience of life similar to that outside the Institute.

You will ask me how we carry out the programme we set? Perhaps you would think that we must have a specific method and to show how we achieve the programme, I will give one lesson as an example. At the beginning of every lesson the first and most important thing is to establish the pre-conditions for success. Every lesson has an introductory section which includes *creating a pleasant atmosphere* and the feeling that the work is fun. This is promoted by the collective dynamic of a well organised group. Also important at this stage is the absolute order in the room, a good general arrangement, right *grouping* and positioning and preparation of the necessary *aids*. Having created the cooperative attitude of the children the conductor establishes a self-conscious *learning situation* and sets up an always clearly understandable goal – however simple it may be. (Do the children know why it is necessary to achieve the goal? Because reaching it is connected to their daily activities, in which they are greatly interested). After this comes the child's *intention* to fulfill the task. Why intention? In automatically occurring everyday functions the sequence of co-ordinated purposeful behaviour occurs automatically, irrespective of whether there is any self-instruction (either thought or verbal).

A dysfunctional person's part-functions do not follow one another in a coordinated way and sequence. Breaking up a task according to the child's ability and stating the intention of achieving these parts separately using rhythm promotes anticipation, the right timing and thus co-ordination. Understanding, intention and voluntary performance of the divided parts of the entire task always precede later involuntary action. (Here I must tell you that this automisation is not the result of passive mechanical connection of a respondent behaviour but the result of a most active operant learning. In repeating most conscious functions some of the part-functions drop out of consciousness). There are some children whose part-functions do not follow one another even if they are separately intended, so the child has to learn the intention corresponding to his action beforehand to execute his own will. The conductor guiding the child makes sure that the intention ensures the right solution (The support that she extends – when the child is already acting voluntarily – results in performance of the task in which the child is independent of her teacher.)

Here I must mention that every performance of a task means that in addition to the achievement of the specific goal and effect difficulties are overcome successfully. The success attained after the intention is brought immediately to the child's consciousness and, of course, the conductor gets the children to make further use of the new ability. The newly performed models or functions are always applied under various conditions in our daily programme. And for this it is ideal if the surroundings are animating, cheerful, encouraging, and deal with various problems, not empty and abstract.

How does the conductor know how to guide the child to success? The conductor teaches and educates and takes care of the most elementary functions that need to be done. She creates interest and attention, informs the children about the tasks and makes sure that these are understood. She guides the children to appropriate solutions and evaluates those solutions and, on the basis of her constant observation, plans further lessons. Here I have to speak about the observation skills of the conductor that are very significant. The conductor does not see the child's dyskinesis only in isolation, she has the chance to observe *all the actions*, day by day, in the course of organised or spontaneous periods. The periods that are not organised, where the child can act spontaneously are the best time for this observation. This observation provides valuable information about improvement and possible further improvement and is most important for the preparation of plans.

The most important *aspect of behaviour* of the conductor is the habit of observing and watching the minds, movements and states of the children. She sees what kind of practical demands there are in life, what can be achieved psychologically, in which position or posture, on which intention and during what time a solution can be achieved, in which stage help is needed, how this support can be decreased or substituted, how faulty reactions can be prevented She combines testing with teaching. She is planning the solution of tasks on the basis of continuous evaluation and making use of every possibility, all displays of spontaneity in guiding the children. The ways and hows of certain performances are different in every child to a small degree but are still of great importance. There cannot therefore be any uniform and concise techniques. On the basis of learnt basic principles, knowledge and objective observation the conductor has to establish the child's ability. She makes suitable plans for lessons and can explain why she has chosen the given solution in the case of each child The conductor is also in an advantageous position because she has the opportunity to make and change her timetable. The time devoted to academic teaching can be fully exploited because there is the possibility to develop abilities required for school-work out of school time.

She controls, designs and guides all the above work. She breaks the whole programme into parts, taking special care of the children's mental and psychological characteristics and organises the entire life of this small community. But this does not mean she is left alone with problems, as there are specialists in every profession who are helping regularly.

On the basis of my lecture one could think that we are dealing with one central aim with the children but the fact is that the children are learning not just to eat as it was shown and they do not practise the ways of standing up all day long nor do we set the single aim of learning to write. The truth is that the children act on the basis of a carefully prepared programme corresponding to the current position of the group and the individuals belonging to it. This work lasts from the moment of waking up until that of going to sleep as per the determined timetable and is directed by the conductor and influenced by the members of the group itself.

4.

Exasperation, 1981

Mária Hári learned French when she was a little girl. She loved the language and French culture, and remained throughout her life more fluent in French than she ever became in English. At this, her second public appearance at a Francophone conference, she needed this ready facility – and she used it.

The original document presented in this chapter has been translated from French. It is not a paper that she herself prepared but a record of what she actually said, a typed transcript by an unknown hand. The written text comes closest of all the materials presented here to the spontaneous and authentic voice of a Hári that those who knew her sometimes knew only too well – angry, indignant, insistent in the defence of the system of Conductive Education that was her life's work, and on the absolute necessity for proper training in this – against those many who persistently failed to grasp its pedagogic essence and promulgated mechanistic alternatives under the same name.

A summary report of the conference and her contribution, subsequently published in a French journal [22] was formal, anodyne. It wholly omitted her fire and frustration but did provide details of the overall event that help one picture the circumstances that occasioned her powerful feelings. She was present as 'President of Honour' of the two-day meeting, billed as 'Study days on the Pető method'. On the first morning there were presentations on the Bobath method, French 'therapeutic education', the Vojta method and the neuropaediatric approach. Only after all that could she speak, knowing from the programme that the second day would be taken up with 'various experiences of integrated re-

---

[22] Anon (1981) Journées d'étude sur la méthode Petö. *Motricite cérébrale*, no.2, pp.92-94.

education...influenced by the Pető method' – from Poland, Japan, Holland, Belgium and England.

Presumably as President of Honour Mária Hári sat on the platform throughout, bemused and angry at what was being presented under the name of the system for which she served as chatelaine, impatient but in the context impotent to do anything about it. This transcript records what she said when she had the opportunity.

Her fundamental point is that Conductive Education is *not* a bundle of methods easily picked up on short courses but a dynamic adaptive pedagogic system requiring extensive and careful professional training. The capitalisation towards the end of her contribution is taken from the original transcript. It suggests not simply emphasis (shown elsewhere in the transcript *in italics*) BUT VERY STRONG EMPHASIS INDEED.

There appear to have been tables prepared to accompany her intended presentation at this conference: only one is mentioned in this transcription but was not included with the text. The films and photographs that were such a bone of contention are also no longer available.

Conductive Education

Transcript of a presentation at the Study Days on the Pető method, Brussels, 1-2 April 1981

I was surprised when I read Conductive Education emphasised in the programme without there really being the time to show it. Excuse me for beginning the lecture by opposing myself to the title of the symposium 'The Pető method'. First, as one sees in the programme, other things will be spoken about; secondly, Conductive Education is much more than a method. This system of education is open to many methods, it is the structure, the organisation of the work, the 'conduction' in the teaching that are its principles – and its result, social integration, is its fundamental characteristic.

The Pető Institute has been working since 1946 and collaborates with numerous disciplines. In 1963 its successes were recognised within education; since that time a government decree created the training of the educators, the 'conductors', and the government has prescribed the creation of a Conductive Education network.

I present you with the result of a systematic survey of all those with motor handicaps of central origin and of those with myopathy from zero to fourteen years. It was carried out by the Pető Institute. According to an analysis of records as at December 1980 this included 7,849 people. We have made a classification of which the criteria are the prospects and the provisions made:

> 2% are dead;
>
> 28% require the care of a health establishment (progressive hydrocephalus, status epilepticus, vegetative state, other cases which interfere with education as therapy);
>
> 5% are myopaths (they require an educational institution

for the whole of their life);

7% are myelodyplegics (they require an educational institution for a very long time);

16% are the responsibility of our Institute.

> 200 children are residential, eighty children are half-boarders. There are many out-patients – outside the Institute building as well: in a hospital and in two homes for young handicapped people and in a district of Budapest, hemiplegics, Parkinsonians, paraplegics and people with head-injuries (adults). The Institute also collaborates with three education centres, a school for motor disorders and with four hospitals for new-borns and babies which we take charge of immediately if they have need. In the Institute there are 150 babies who come each day with their parents as out-patients.

32% (2905), a very big percentage, have become integrated through Conductive Education.

> They go on foot to normal school or to special school (not special school for children with motor disorder) or they already attend secondary school, university or even they already work. Another diagram shows by age groups the dimension of the integrated children.

17% are excluded from school because of a supposed shortcoming, solely because of diagnosis;

3% do not go to school because the distance is too great;

3% differ in some degree in their performance in

writing, in speech etc – these latter and the 5% who are left have still to be helped.

In conclusion: the proportion of those who have been integrated is very large, the necessary number of educators is relatively restricted. The results were very good, Conductive Education is one solution to the problem. That is why to solve it one of the state's first measures was the introduction of conductor-training. A method can be learned during a course but *the system of Conductive Education cannot be applied other than by conductors* who have received a training in Conductive Education of four years. *The quality of the results of Conductive Education is conditional upon the quality of the conductors' training*

The elements of Conductive Education can be likened to the elements of some known methods like those of the analytic and global therapies. All the elements can be found with us but the basis of the whole programme is pedagogic. The conductor's principle merit is to orchestrate well the process of a hierarchical whole. She can give preference to one point or another, she chooses the methods, the dose, the graduation, the combinations. The long training is done in service, participating responsibly in the work. The conductor learns various specialisms and assimulates acquisitions which have certain and practical value within a unity, modifying them according to the principle of Conductive Education. Later the conductor can specialise but she remains the generalist conductor who is a child specialist. No specialist could be a conductor without the four years of integrated education for conductors. So you must understand that *what is called Conductive Education* or the Pető method at this symposium *is certainly not it!* The generalists and the specialists are not opposed to each other, no more than are synthesis and analysis. One asks and one listens to the specialists but it is the conductor who realises the whole with her synthetic view.

The work of the team, individual and individualised work are no longer opposed to each other. It is in the team that individualisation is easiest to realise.

Since the time of the film showing the work and its structure over a day would take fifty minutes, and I do not have the necessary time, I am not going to show more than the first half: the group of mothers and their children. It is a cross-sectional image, which shows the teaching of the parents.

Response to questions

By choice, I would like to respond by showing the film that I have brought, which shows the integrated work of one day and with all the little films which show the structure of the series of tasks and the structure of a group made up of different children, but although the symposium is called 'Pető days' there is no time to show them. So I will make a verbal response.

1. Conductive Education is not straight functionalism. The goal of the educator is not reduced to the execution of functions. If one wished to execute the functions directly that would be a failure (like with you) because one cannot exercise something that does not exist. In Conductive Education there are several phases. An important phase is the development of coordination and another is the application of the coordination that has been developed. The same person develops something and applies it when the opportunity arises during the day. Functioning without applying the coordination that has been learned, that is to say dysfunction, leads to nothing of benefit.

2. Conductive Education is as complex as education itself. If education is good, if one is not making a mechanical display instead of education, then one has no need of technical rigour to ensure employment of the coordinations that have been learned (the important things: human contact, emotion, interest, curiosity, confidence, the requirements of the community, affective emotion). Reafferentation of the attained objective brings positive emotions, lack of success – frustration. Lack of time is also accompanied by negative emotions. All these things are purely pedagogic and psychological. The child depends upon the security and the

70

harmony of the conductor who attributes the achievement to his initiatives and not to the one who treats him. The subject is motivated to do well. The work of the conductor is simply to motivate the child to do well. The angle of attack is not the musculature nor the reflex mechanism, nor some part of the nervous system that we know remarkably well but not well enough. The angle of attack is the personality, the morale. The explanation of sessions in Conductive Education overlaps with the area of functions, gestures, the explanation is in the pedagogical and psychological domain. It is necessary to study Conductive Education in order to do, in the same way as it is necessary to study pedagogy or music to do it.

3. Verbal accompaniment of what we make ourselves do is not simply what Luriya has described, it is much more: by using the word one learns to coordinate the intention with the execution. The strength of the will would increase spasticity and dyskinesis, incorrect intention would provoke the opposite to the intention and the disillusion that would follow it would fettle the will. One can indeed learn despite spasticity. This is an essential point, that one learns to wish in order to have success. In this learning the tasks that we do, the series of exercises, have didactic importance. They are realisable by employing suitable coordination, they have as their end the experience of intention and its correlation with its realisation. The resolved task is not a mechanical practice but training in methods of problem-solving (Bernshtein) As I have said it would be necessary to have the time to demonstrate this with the films.

4. The series of tasks lead successively to the goal. They have didactic importance. From the start to the end of the series all the tasks must serve our goals. We approach having the goals realised through breaking down the functions, lengthening various phases in order to be able to control the beginning, the middle, the end, the speed and the dynamism. They lead indirectly to experience of less effort. What has been achieved in one task will be employed in the next and each successive task will be more complex.

5. The conductor knows the possibilities, the complementary aids, the detailed coordinates of all the children and in no way exceeds their capacities. Each action of their daily life is required in an individualized and elaborated form. The child learns that he can change position. The conductor must prove it to him. The conductor gives him the chance to interact with the environment and to overcome difficulties. The programmes have didactic importance. The timetable must ensure the time necessary to do something well. It is only in the framework of such a programme that we can attain our goals. THE ONLY CONCLUSION OF THIS SYMPOSIUM is that if one wishes to have the results that we have, it is necessary to learn conduction.

I have brought all the films that are important for explanation. Out of this *embarrass de richesse,* given the lack of time, I am not choosing the big film on the integration of the programme of the day but two extremes from the series of tasks: one before the leaving and one at the beginning for children who do not know either how to speak nor even to sit, then I show how we document what each child learns in order to walk. There are more than ten thousand series of tasks which one must learn in order to choose well.

5.

Out East, 1981

Throughout the Socialist period there was no take-up of Conductive Education in the Soviet Bloc, not least because other than in Hungary motor-disordered children and adults were not a subject of intellectual interest or social provision in those countries. In the early nineteen-seventies there had been a fact-finding visit to Mária Hári's Institute from the premier East European research establishment in the field of special education, the Institute of Defectology in Moscow, which resulted in publication of a brief but comprehensive account of 'conductive upbringing'[23] which spoke favourably of what was being done. There has been no further practical interest beyond continuation of a long tradition of receiving occasional individual clients from the 'fraternal republics' (stretching right back to Andras Pető's earliest days[24]) – with an especial welcome for ethnic Hungarians from neighbouring states.

It is perhaps surprising therefore to find that in 1981 Mária Hári travelled East of Moscow to the fairly distant Russian city of Suzdal' to speak at an international Eastern Bloc conference.. There was little love lost between most Hungarians and the Soviet Union and it might be that her visit was occasioned by official invitation to the Hungarian Heath Ministry for contributions to a prestigious event.

Even more so than in the two papers that Mária Hári read at Wallingford thirteen years before, during her first visit to the West, her paper presented at Suzdal' was a concentrated, systematised summary of the theory and practice of Conductive Education – and

---

[23] Semenova, K. and E. Mastyukova, E. (1974) On the conductive upbringing of children with cerebral palsies in the Hungarian People's republic [in Russian], *Defectologiya*, no 2, 93-95.

[24] Ákos,K. and Ákos, M. (1997) The enigmatic Dr Pető. *The Conductor*,6(3-4), pp.49-55.

similarly excessive for oral presentation to an audience most of whom would have known little or nothing of the orientation and work of her institute or even necessarily about rehabilitation of children with motor disorders. Like those earlier papers, this formal presentation bears the marks of very careful preparation, not just in its translation but in its analysis and systematisation. It offers nothing substantitively new – hardly necessary in the circumstances – but a certain commonality of theoretical position across the Bloc and (if the presumption of 'official' involvement in her being there is justified) possible official vetting of what she was to say make this paper Mária Hári's tightest statement of Conductive Education and its pedagogy yet identified.

This tightness of expression makes for a bold and authoritative statement but the paper's general tone (it reads very much like a Soviet technical paper of the time) means that its strengths may be lost to today's Western readers. We do not know how her audience received it but there appear to have been no further publications in Russian (other than her own follow-up paper in the *Korsakov Journal*, mentioned below) nor any institutional contact with the impecunious countries of the Eastern Bloc over the final decade of the Socialist era, over which period Mária Hári and her Institute, in advance of Hungary as a whole, were becoming more and more embroiled with the Capitalist West.

Her concluding plea for wider and deeper appreciation of the basis of Conductive Education is, however, compatible with the emerging new orientation to spreading the word, as noted in the introduction to the previous chapter and presages the heartfelt plea that concludes her final paper presented in this book.

Whether or not Mária Hári could read Russian she was unable to speak it with ease. The English translation published here has been translated from a formal paper typed in competent technical Russian – specially prepared for reading aloud by someone who was far from fluent in that language. We do not know how her paper went on the day. One hopes that everything went to plan at such an important and formal event, unlike what happened in Brussels six months earlier, permitting her to show her photos and film as she had intended. Neither was available here but her account of then, so characteristic of how she liked to present, has been retained.

Russian spelling is very regular, corresponding closely to the spoken word. Given a little rehearsal, anyone who knows the thirty-four letters of the Russian alphabet should be able to stumble laboriously through reading a short Russian text aloud. There is, however, a catch. The stress (that is the emphasis) on the various syllables of Russian words is *very* strong and notoriously variable from word to word (very unlike Hungarian with its invariably stressed first syllable). Stressing the wrong syllable can seriously affect the intelligibility and the meaning of what is said. With a single exception there is no written indication of where the stress falls nor are there any rules or regulations, one just has to know from experience. Mária Hári did not have this experience and someone with a neat and precise hand (certainly not Mária Hári's!) carefully inked in a stress mark over the dominant syllable of every word in the typewritten script. Perhaps then, reading this paper at a formal conference in a distant Soviet city may have been quite a stressful experience in more senses than one.

Mária Hári's exposition fits easily into the conceptual framework of Soviet practitioners of the time. Her opening sentence, summarizing the content of what she is about to say, does not so much imply 'how children with athetosis develop' as how *we* develop *them.* Remember too the particular emphasis for Soviet (and fraternal) psycho-pedagogues of the words translated here as 'teaching' and 'development'.

The congruity between the Hungarian word *nevelés* and the Russian *vospitanie* has been maintained in this chapter, using the term 'conductive upbringing' instead of the (to us) more familiar Conductive Education to convey some of the sense of how readily comprehensible the text that she read at Suzdal' would appear to a Soviet audience. Her use of the word 'reafferentation' would have been another firm point of reference at this Eastern Bloc neurological conference. The Soviet physiologist N. I. Bernshtein had been known in psychology in the West as well as the Soviet Bloc through his 'cognitive physiology', which emphasised the role of feedback, purpose and future consequences in the control of movement. Not surprisingly therefore Mária Hári often cited him to help explain Conductive Education. Reafferentation is an important feature of Bernshtein's theories.

The Russian manuscript mentions but does not include a table. The conference in Suzdal' occurred in October 1981. Not long after she published a paper, also in Russian, in the *Korsakov Journal of Neuropathology and Psychiatry*[25]. This differed in content from the paper read in Suzdal', addressing Conductive Education more generally than just for athetoid children, but did include a table that appears to cover the same ground and is therefore included here. It also included grainy photographs of children but these illustrated points other than those that she was making in Suzdal'.

---

[25] M. Hari (1982) The method of conductive upbringing and its role in the social adaptation of children suffering from cerebral palsy [in Russian]. *Korsakov Journal of Neuropathology and Psychiatry*, 82(10), pp.1507-1510.

The conductive upbringing of children with double athetosis

Paper read to the Symposium of the Socialist Countries on Child Neurology, Suzdal', 5-6 October 1981

Esteemed chairman!

Esteemed audience!

My brief report contains a description of the development of athetoid children.

As a result of conductive upbringing the athetoid child learns to restrain his involuntary movements, keep his balance and manifest purposeful actions in time and space. As a result of this he becomes capable of mastering school learning material and, in the long run, performing socially useful labour.

Mastery of coordination applies also to speech and to writing.

One must not exclude the teaching of speech and writing from the process of upbringing, indeed it is useless to do so, one must not replace them with electronic means or employ symbols.

The upbringing of athetoid children must include the same basic principles of pedagogy as in the upbringing and teaching of normal children. These basic principles are also used in the system of conductive upbringing. The difference between the upbringing and teaching of normal children and conductive upbringing is solely the break-down of tasks for each child into parts, depending upon his level in movement, speech and other functions. For example, with respect to breaking down tasks, if the child's leg jerks up involuntarily when he makes an action or intends to make one, then one must teach him to keep his leg consciously in a calm condition when making any prescribed movement. As a result of such a system of teaching he is already walking independently, his leg does not jump up and he does not fall on his back.

Each child in the process of fufilling his own task forms his own individual, orthofunctionally acting capabilities. The specialist teacher, the conductor, renders help in the course of performing the series of tasks on the teaching programme so that the child forms the coordination appropriate for him, masters it and reinforces it. To ensure appropriate help it is necessary to evaluate the changing conditions daily and, according to the child's development, even to introduce frequent corrections to the programme as necessary.

The conductor creates inter-communication and an active atmosphere, activates and then directs this level of activity that she has created and utilises it. The conductor's most basic, most general aim, is the creation of initiative. The crux of the matter is to call into life a truly purposeful energy, as a result of which is created a single purpose, the ability to construct a goal-directed, high-quality system, so that the child's upbringing should not have the fragmentation of many specialists with their own various aims. This energy, on which we depend in the above system of upbringing, can be created only in such an atmosphere. The child's energy, his anticipation and the manifestation of his will are not in themselves enough. If his will is mistakenly directed, then this will increase spasms and excessive movements, as a consequence of which he will not perform successfully, and this lack of success in its turn exerts adverse reaction upon the will, it impedes it. The conductor, the teacher who leads, on the one hand helps the child achieve success and on the other teaches the correct manifestation of the child's will and entails the correct way.

The conductor takes a series of tasks which have didactic significance. In these the aims of each separate task – which can be verified by way of concrete feedback – are achievable only by correct coordination. Thus, each task of this series serves the formation of correct coordination and consequently the correct connection of intention and its performance. Such tasks constitute quite small and consciously well controlled elements of more complex functions and may be mastered without spasms and excessive movements. They can be combined into a series of tasks and attached to each movement and position.

On the basis of the data Table 1, about two thousand children were discharged from our Institute over ten years, out of which on average 72% successfully learned to adapt to the conditions of general kinder-gartens, schools and workplaces.

Year	Overall number of children treated	Number of successful cases	
		Absolute	Percentage
1970	226	163	72.4
1971	156	113	72.4
1972	209	158	75.5
1973	186	142	76.3
1974	261	186	71.2
1975	244	157	64.3
1976	201	135	61.1
1977	179	114	63.6
1978	137	114	83.2
1979	133	104	78.1

Table 1: Effectiveness of restorative therapy in nervous-system disease in children[26]

---

[26] Taken from *Korsakov Journal of Neuropathology and Psychiatry*, 82 (10), p.68, maintaining the terminology of the original

Although the training of conductor-pedagogues to a large extent solves the problem of athetoid children, the transition to the collective of the normal or the special school presents serious difficulty all the same. The long path followed, essential to achieve the results gained, is not always valued as it should be.

The athetoid school-child always develops further in the school collective and, even after receiving the school-leaving certificate, develops his speech and writing further, becomes someone capable of work, able to associate in society if he receives support in the long term.

The training and retraining of parents and teachers are essential in the interests of school integration, also a swifter pace in broadcasting knowledge of the theory and practice of the network of conductive upbringing and also giving help to assist its wider dissemination.

6.

On the back foot, 1990

By 1990 when this paper was written Conductive Education, the
Pető Institute – and Mária Hári herself – had been catapulted into
world attention by the phenomenon of the TV documentary
Standing up for Joe and its aftermath, the unprecedented influx of
families with children with motor disorders, travelling across the
Iron Curtain to Budapest. One outcome of this phenomenon was a
new kind of interest in Conductive Education from professionals
outside Hungary, some of it a genuine and kindly enquiry into
what lay behind the popular enthusiasm, some defensive. Over the
nineteen-eighties interest from abroad, from a new generation of
activists and the popular media and political feeding frenzy that
followed in their wake, had pushed aside criticism in Hungary
itself. The extraordinary and altogether unexpected effect of this
was that the Pető Institute (as it had been renamed in 1985) came
for a time to be regarded in Hungary as a valuable national asset, at
the forefront of privatisation and considered unquestionably
deserving of major financial support from foreign governments.

In the wake of the families, reporters and politicians who flocked
to Budapest following *Standing up for Joe* – almost all of them
returning home to express their unqualified enthusiasm – came
inevitably a cavalcade of professional visitors on fact-finding
missions, and a more critical and technical attention to Conductive
Education than it had hitherto received. One way in which the
Pető Institute managed the volume of requests for visits and
information was to run a one-week course for foreign
paediatricians, which was held in June 1988.

Three of the participants on this course, from the Chailey Heritage
Hospital in England, later wrote a report on their conclusions and
observations, based upon their observations at the Pető Institute
and what they had been told there. The following Summer this

was accepted for publication by the *British Medical Journal*, their paper being finally published in November 1989.[27] Their overall conclusion on the outcomes of Conductive Education at the Pető Institute were carefully phrased but nonetheless damaging to claims for the relative benefit of this system:

> '...we conclude that a minority of selected children with cerebral palsy and spina bifida who have a relatively good prognosis are educated at the Institute... and the children probably fare better as a result of the intensive programme than do children in Britain in areas where therapy is scarce. They seem to achieve, however, what we would expect similar children in Britain to do where facilities are adequate.'

Their report granted favourable attention to the conductive system itself, concluding as follows:

> 'The role of the conductor and the integration of programmes into a classroom setting have much to recommend them and Conductive Education, if successfully transferred to Britain, might be beneficial to a wider range of children than in Hungary.'

Both conclusions were taken up in the guest editorial of that issue of the *British Medical Journal* [28], which went on to extol recent developments of orthopaedic surgery and early physiotherapy. Both articles in the *British Medical Journal* were then reported in the widely read *Therapy Weekly*, with brief note of the role of the conductor and emphasis upon the judgment about comparative outcomes and encouragement of 'physiotherapy up to the age of seven'. [29]

---

[27] Robinson, R. O., McCarthy, G.T., Little, T.M. (1989) Conductive Education at the Pető Institute, Budapest. *British Medical Journal*, 299, pp. 1145-49

[28] Patrick, J. (1989) Cerebral palsy diplegia: improvements for walking. Much publicity about Hungarian methods ignores developments in Britain.. *British Medical Journal*, 299, pp. 1115-6

[29] British methods 'as good as Peto'. (1989) *Therapy Weekly*, 6 (17), pp, 9, 11

This was much more than simply a matter of professional debate. It was also political, both in the United Kingdom and in Hungary. Only a week before publication of the two articles in the *British Medical Journal* the UK government had announced new regulations to permit local education authorities to fund children to go overseas for specialist help for their special educational needs – this in direct response to the Pető phenomenon. This was not taken well by many professionals and authorities in the UK who considered that such resources would be better spent at home. For Mária Hári in Budapest the articles posed a political problem of a different kind. She was by now no longer director of a state institution but responsible to the commercially oriented board of a non-profit company. In March 1989 this board launched a domestically high-profile international appeal which aimed mainly at foreign governments, intending to raise US$60 million to build an enormous international institute. The report and editorial in the *British Medical Journal*, one of the world's most prestigious and authoritative medical publications must have come later that year as a public-relations and marketing disaster. Someone would have to make reply.

Anna-Maria McGee visited the Pető Institute early in 1990 and found Mária Hári exceedingly unwelcoming and, despite it being a previously made arrangement, initially adamant that this professional visitor from the United Kingdom would in no circumstances be 'permished' (another familiar Hári-ism) to observe work in a group. Admission was negotiated only when Anna-Marie McGee traded an agreement to give final proof-reading to an article that Mária Hári was about to submit to the *British Medical Journal* in response to the report published a few months before. The article was already prepared in English and looked like having been worked upon by an English-speaker: in the event it proved very hard to get Mária Hári to change anything except the most minor detail.

This is the article published in this chapter. As it stands it is not publishable and it never in fact appeared in the *British Medical Journal*. It is not know whether it was in fact submitted. The *British Medical Journal* does not retain records.

How did the three paediatricians arrive at their comparative opinion? Perhaps they were not told that children who were unlikely to make it out of the Pető Institute into a local elementary school were educated in the 'old' Institute in Villányi út: certainly foreign visitors were never taken there to see children who spent the whole of their school years at the Pető Institute – even though the work at Villányi út was both excellent and interesting. And even in the smart new showcase building in Kútvúlgyi út visitors did not always realize that there were groups and sub-groups that were not shown. It was inevitable that a policy of emphasizing the high-achieving should back-fire in accusation of selectivity. Never mind what they saw though, and the impressions that this gave, discerning visitors still wanted to know about the wider facts about childhood motor disorder in Hungary and the Pető Institute's place in providing for this. A most detailed record of that paediatricians' course in June 1988 was made by Carole McCracken, a New Zealand participant [30], not herself a paediatrician but the mother of a child with Down's syndrome, who took up the place of a New Zealand paediatrician who had suddenly died. Her notes show the lectures accompanied by a blizzard of statistics and the very first question from the floor being 'How are the children selected?' Unfortunately the statistics were of the same tantalizing nature as those that she used in her conference presentations and Mária Hári could not answer the question of selectivity. Data from these statistics were used to make the authors' point in the article that appeared in the *British Medical Journal.*

Mária Hári was stung by what she regarded as the totally unfair accusation of selecting only those children for Conductive Education who could be expected to succeed anyway – though, truth to tell, were this the case it offered an extraordinary accolade for her Institute's power of prediction. Her response provides an interesting account of the organisation of the Institute and of the arrangements for initial selection, written in the wider context of provision for disabled children in Hungary at that time, but she responded to the statistical challenge by more of the same, statistics which do not answer the wider epidemiological point. An

---

[30] McCracken, C. (1988) Notes on lectures given at the one-week course for paediatricians, Pető Institute, June 1988

opportunity was missed to pursue Hungary's surprisingly complex provision of special education and habilitation for disabled children (though Anna-Marie McGee[31] later tried) and more importantly open up a debate between Conductive Education and professionals in the West.

This debate never happened. In one way this no longer mattered because the old East–West divide was ready to make way for a new order. Already in September 1989 the Hungarian government had opened its Western frontiers to refugees from East Germany. The regimes of Eastern Europe collapsed one after the other and within two years the Cold War was over. There was no longer need for the UK government to maintain its foreign-policy interest in extending its support for the Pető Institute. Conductive Education was already in a 'transitional' phase anyway [32]and the trickle of conductors from the Pető Institute off to seek their fortune in the West became a flood. Within a few years these *émigré* conductors were demonstrating very concretely the correctness of the visiting paediatricians' point that 'Conductive Education, if successfully transferred to Britain, might be beneficial to a wider range of children than in Hungary', in a considerably greater range of countries worldwide, and it began slowly to dawn that in future there would be more to Conductive Education than what had been done at the Pető Institute under Socialism.

The epidemiological issue remained unresolved.

---

[31] McGee, A.-M. (1990) Short report, Mexikói út: a special school in Hungary. *European Journal of Special Needs Education*, 5 (3) 231-4 and (1992) A stitch in time. *Therapy Weekly*, 14 May, p.6.

[32] Read, J. (1992) *Conductive Education, 1987-93: the transitional years.* Birmingham: Foundation for Conductive Education

The Pető System of Conductive Education

Manuscript prepared for submission to the British Medical Journal, March 1990

Introduction

Reading about rehabilitation one finds a number of studies defining the same goals, the maximum possible development for the disabled person and his integration into society. Emphasis is often placed upon early recognition and upon multidisciplinary treatment. Despite these efforts, however, a considerable number of patients do not achieve the expected level of development. In some cases educational gain seems impossible. There is a tendency to develop objective prognostic tools to provide explanatory statements for the possible delay in achievements and there are also claims that some outcomes do not justify the negative prognoses associated with them. A fundamental change in the approach to rehabilitation brought about by an entirely new educational system, Conductive Education, has demonstrated the possibility of further development for some motor disordered children and adults through learning.

To evaluate the efficacy of Conductive Education we must ask whether the apparent development of the child could be explained by chance and therefore not be significant. Reference to this question was made in a previous article (Robinson, *et al*) which stated that the outcomes observed may be due to the degree to which children with less severe impairment are selected for Conductive Education and not related to the originality of the educational programme that they receive at the Pető Institute. In this *BMJ* article Dr Robinson describes his hypothesis about selective assessment as follows:

> a minority of carefully selected children with
> cerebral palsy and spina bifida who have a

> relatively good prognosis are educated at the institute.

Elsewhere the same writer stresses:

> the actual content of the programme may have little new to offer to the experienced therapist.

If the children selected are those with good prognosis then the originality or otherwise of the programme is not relevant, as it might be argued that such children would be likely to develop in any case. If, however, the children attending the Pető Institute are *not* stringently selected then the content and nature of the programme which is provided for them is a matter of interest. This article attempts to provide answers to the questions about the outcomes and principles of the Pető system's 'Conductive Education'.

Initial assessment and admission

Traditionally, assessment is the most essential starting point of every step taken in the management of motor-disordered children. It has important predictive elements based on the hypothesis that children initially found to be severely impaired will develop less successfully and has an equally important diagnostic purpose: to determine which forms of therapy and education might be appropriate. Usually assessment is made by several professionals, primarily by physicians. Here, however, initial assessment, called consultation, which is an important aspect of the integrated Pető system, has less prognostic value. It is not the purpose of the assessment to select chosen therapies, rather at the Pető Institute there is a shift to a primarily educational emphasis.

The consulting conductor shows the person who is seen that he/she is capable of development; motivates this and explains the process of *learning* which will be needed in the future. This assessment determines the educationally appropriate group to which the child will be allocated within the system. The other part of the initial assessment is done by specialist doctors – for contra-indications, if there are any, to starting work in the groups. Naturally there must also be a primary differentiation of disabilities which do not come within the scope of the Institute. These are motor disabilities of peripheral neural origin, of orthopaedic or rheumathologic origin, and muscle diseases. Those children who are primarily mentally retarded, deaf or blind require special education and are allocated accordingly. Children who are profoundly mentally retarded and older than three years, and those who need medical treatment have to be sent to nursing homes and hospitals. For blind cerebrally palsied children there is a special institution where a conductor (trained by us) works in a team in a special programme for the blind.

Number and percentage assessed	Findings
215 80.6%	Admitted to groups
32 11.94%	Advised to be treated by orthopaedic and physiotherapeutic means
16 5.97%	Found primarily profoundly mentally handicapped
1 0.37%	Found to be blind
2 0.75%	Only deaf
1 0.37%	Only behavioural problems

Table 1: Data for 268 children presented [for initial assessment] in the first part of 1989

For profoundly mentally handicapped children who are cerebrally palsied but ineducable and who are placed in residential care for their whole lives there are only one or two institutions where conductors are asked to or are in a position to give some help in their management. Based upon current data an example of the first assessment is shown in Table 1.

The assessments on admitted children follow over several months. They are done partly by the Institute medical section, with specialist contributions from three paediatricians, two neurologists, two internists, two opthalmologists, two orthopaedists, one audiologist, one otorhinolaryngologist, one urologist, one dermatologist, one dentist and one psychologist, and also through connection with special hospitals and clinics.

Referral and registration

It is important to say that in Hungary all newborns with problems are assessed outside the Institute, in their local hospitals, in their local districts or in central clinics, by neuropaediatricians and their teams who decide about interventions other than the Pető system. There is no compulsory screening and no compulsion to bring the child to the Institute if a motor problem is detected. Our information about the children is supplied partly by the community paediatrician, who has to tell the Institute if he knows of a child in need in his own county, and also by children's hospitals. Children are also brought to us directly by their parents. This explains that, whilst the age range in which children are presented at the Institute is much lower than ten years ago, even today there is a difference between the number of known children in the age ranges 0–5 and 6–10. For the last thirty-six years the data on all known cerebrally palsied or spina bifida children under fourteen years have been registered. Table 2 shows the proportions of these children in December 1988.

Children who have none of the contra-indications outlined earlier are admitted for conduction. The December 1988 statistics show that out of 9,772 people assessed 7,016 (71.8%) were admitted. (although this proportion differs in different age range groups – see Table 3.)

Age range	Number registered
0-5	1,171
6-10	2,015
11.15	1,885
16-20	1,453
21-25	1,264
26-30	938
31-36	1,046

Table 2: Proportions of known persons in age groups, in December 1988

Number of children assessed	Age groups	Number of children admitted	Percentage of children admitted
1,171	0-5	1,016	87.76%
2,015	6-10	1,502	74.54%
1,885	11-15	1,355	71.88%
1,453	16-20	977	55.74%
1,264	21-25	855	70.02%
938	26-30	560	59.70%
1,046	31-36	716	68.45%
9,772	0-36	7,016	71.80%

Table 3: Proportion of children admitted in different age groups, December 1988

Robinson *et al* state that the children whom we admit are those who have a relatively good prognosis: then 72% of the identified Hungarian cerebral palsied and spina bifida populations must have a relatively good prognosis.

This clearly cannot be the case. Further, if we examine the tables presented, it is clear that the statement that only 'a minority of carefully selected children' are educated at the Institute must also be untrue.

It is also most important for visitors to the Pető Institute to recognise that before making any assumptions about the 'relatively mild' cases of cerebral palsy and spina bifida whom they observe, they must understand which stage in the education process they are observing. The apparent 'mildness' of the handicapping condition may be due to the success of the programme and not reflect the original severity at all.

Contiguity in conduction and long-term outcome

At the moment 1,546 children and approximately three hundred adults are educated in the Institute. Five hundred of these are residents and the remaining children and adults are seen in our outpatients' department. Adults and children from other countries are not included in these figures. The departments are not a set of separately functioning entities, they form a unified system. Continual re-evaluations, transmissions, exchanges and intercommunications ensure continuity of conduction. A large number of children who are developing well do not need to become residential. A smaller number develop more slowly and become residential because of their slower progress. At admission as residents, should this prove necessary, children will have two to four years of Conductive Education behind them. Many of these children who come from the outpatients' department will become pupils in the school and are prepared for this move in our own kindergarten. The children leaving the Institute are monitored by their own group leader for one year and are then monitored by the aftercare department. The aftercare and follow-up departments work continually with people who have become integrated into society and also with people who required long-term placements in institutions. These departments check the transition to schools and work and also organise any help necessary.

Age group	Number of assessed children	Number of admitted children	Left	MR (%)	I	L	O	E	?
0-5	1,171	1,016	249	205 (82.33%)	-	28	6	9	1
6-10	2,015	1,502	1,015	889 (87.59%)	19	49	1	33	14
11-15	1,885	1,355	1,159	1,026 (88.52%)	16	60	21	27	9
16-20	1,453	977	934	695 (74.41%)	28	147	31	23	0
21-25	1,264	855	867	587 (67.7%)	20	207	20	12	21
26-30	938	560	549	351 (63.93%)	17	137	21	6	17
31-36	1,046	716	698	427 (61.17%)	19	173	11	4	64
	9,772	7,016	5,471	4,180 (76.4%)	119	801	121	114	136

Table 4: Outcomes by age groups and in total

MR = left with maximal result

I = educational subnormal with good ADL

L = less result, longer placement needed

O = in institution for welfare

E = poor result, but developing, placement needed for life

? = no information available

In 1989 we obtained information from eight hundred personal interviews and from written answers to questionnaires. Among the eight hundred cases personally seen only four had any substantial continuing problems. As Table 4 shows, the rate of positive outcome (integration) is 76% and out of 2,423 children in the 0-15 age group this is over 80 %. Table 4 also lists the positive and negative outcomes in specific age groups.

Orthofunction and dysfunction

Some clarification of the confusion that has developed about these terms would seem to be required. Orthofunction is a sort of 'good arrangement' of movement and cognition, responsible for the ability to realise one's intended actions. It is an active organisation of function which is both dynamic and complex. This complicated phenomenon is modified continuously, day to day, by learning, though we are unaware of it. To be 'orthofunctional' relates to learning and depends upon the complex development of personality. It means to be ready to cope with the requirements of the world.

Dysfunction therefore is the term for an inappropriate arrangement of function within the person, in other words poor co-ordination, poor organisation and poor micropattern. Dysfunction can, however, be rearranged and reorganised. Reorganisation consists of *learning how to realise the will.* The means by which the will is realised is cognitive although the child may be aware *only of the goal of his or her actions* and not of their organisation. Such a rearrangement is an evolving process which occurs through learning and is relatively independent of the structural disability.

The objective of Conductive Education is to teach children to learn the organisational process and not merely a performance. Learning is provided by all the previously described parts of the system and by the structured, complex, and unified education that the children receive. Subjects within the curriculum (which includes primary school and kindergarten subjects, sensory and perceptual functions, language, speech and other forms of communication) are incorporated in a systematic framework which supplies a context for them. They must have meaning for the child and logically developed sequences within the structure are given meaning by the context in which they are presented. The conductor has to provide this meaning for the child's conscious learning. Conduction provides the child with normal subject content, normal education, normal life situations and normal social situations. The subjects have to be related and each subject has to contain a series of goals in *simultaneous interconnection*. This *simultaneous* aspect is a new dimension to the education of the motor disordered. The programme is based on *all* the elements in interaction. The subjects do not contain merely a set of elements forming a linear process but are interdependent. Although the subjects and actions differ in content, orthofunction will be uniform in each. This is an essential aspect of the approach. It ensures continuity, unifies a number of subjects and thus generates a new style. The micropattern learned becomes an example for the child and by being involved in more complex processes can eventually be applied to an infinite range of actions and situations. The sequence of different subjects serves the repetition of orthofunction. They are primarily a means to the end of learning orthofunction within different modalities. This is why the concept of the integrity of the Pető method cannot be explained in the quantitative terms of multidisciplinarity.

Outsiders fail to take account of the intensive observation, planning and preparatory function of the conductor whose professional training is the most fundamental aspect, the Gordian knot in realising the Pető system. The observation, planning, structuring and leading functions of the conductor form 'conduction' and as there are many thousands of permutations of factors and situations, there are therefore many thousands of methods. The children have to discover for themselves the solution for realising their goals (active discovery learning) but this needs far more pre-planning than most people are aware of. Behind the conductor's observation lies a host of problems. Correct planning and structuring are the most essential parts of the system, all connections and passages must be pre-planned. The conductor must accentuate personality development, must have a perception of the child's attitude and has to enter into rapport with her pupils. She breaks down barriers between people and facilitates the development of peer-group relationships. She has to present what is to be learnt concretely and understandably. She has to integrate cognitively redundant information into meaningful actions, to bring about affective experience, emotional motivation and a feeling of success. As conduction means to find the way to the known goal and to help children and their families to learn how to achieve this, alternative methods can be chosen. Provided that acceptance into school and job is eventually achieved it does not matter whether this success is achieved in wheelchairs or without, using computerised help or not. The reason we prefer maximum activity is not that we 'haven't any wheelchairs' or that 'Hungarian schools do not accept wheelchair-bound children' but that most children need the achievement of objectives and intentional activities to have the experiences necessary for their perceptual and cognitive development. In these cases help given too early, in the form of mechanical aids, becomes the main obstacle to these essential experiences.

The profession of the conductor is special, based as it is upon this different philosophy and a qualitatively different knowledge base. The answer to the question 'who should be subjected to this system?' is surely not those who benefit from ordinary treatment. The implications of the results that we have obtained have given us insight into further possibilities of personal development. This understanding could perhaps influence future decisions about how best to maximise the potential of motor-disordered children.

To conclude this account of the Pető system, I hope that I have reduced some of the confusion about terminology. What is unusual in this system is its insistence upon unbroken interdependency with structure, rather than upon single methods. Most importantly, it is a system of *education.*

7.

Diplomacy, 1997

In 1993 Mária Hári retired as Director of the Pető Institute though she retained a visiting position, and continued to work there, despite increasing ill-health, teaching students and editing till the summer before she died.

In 1997 Mária Hári attended the First World Congress on Neurodevelopmental Treatment Concept (that is, for readers in the United Kingdom, on the 'Bobath method'), held in Ljubljana in Slovenia, contributing to a short symposium called 'Towards understanding of two other treatment approaches'. The other contribution to this symposium was entitled 'Vojta with Bobath eyes: a look at the Bobath-Vojta working group', reporting on a real attempt at rapprochement. Mária Hári had a lifetime's history of being highly critical of therapists, many of whom had a Bobath orientation. Following the Bobaths' own single visit to see András Pető's work themselves, Karl Bobath had noted: 'The work is good and impressive... the only other approach which makes sense to me other than my own' but tempered this sharply: 'Their claims are exaggerated, in fact their claims are really their aims' [33].

This conference was neither the time nor the place to exchange brickbats and a certain 'diplomatic' approach was called for. Mária Hári achieved this by making a historical comparison between András Pető and the Bobaths and providing a descriptive formulation of the similarities and differences between the two approaches. One could, should one wish, interpret from her concluding quotations from Berta Bobath which approach had the more to learn from the other. This carefully anodyne comparison is a long way from the sharp distinction that she would make in other contexts between Conductive Education and all the 'therapies'.

---

[33] Bobath, K. (1966) Visit to Dr Pető, Budapest (3 days September 1966).Unpublished notes

Conductive Education was a total paradigm shift, and she held true to this to the end of her life.

The English-language typescript from which this paper has been taken is very disorganised and though it does look in places like help was given by an English-speaker, seems more in the way of being a speaker's note rather than a script for oral presentation. In transforming it into a written paper it has still been possible to retain nearly all the text and argument.

Neuro-developmental treatment and Conductive Education

Paper read at the First World Congress of the Neuro-developmental Treatment Concept, Ljubljana, 13–16 June, 1997

Bobath and Pető were the twentieth century's earliest pioneers in the treatment of conditions involving the upper motor neuron of the CNS, for those who had not responded to orthodox treatment. The Bobaths' ideas have been some of the most influential in rehabilitation and Pető has also influenced rehabilitation and education. There are similarities in their life histories, in their thinking and their approach.

Karel Bobath, born in Prague in 1907, trained as a doctor, Berta Bobath born in Berlin in 1908, trained as remedial gymnast. Pető, born in Szombathely, fourteen years earlier in 1893, trained as a doctor in Vienna, became a tuberculosis specialist and a neuropsychiatrist, and then began to work in rehabilitation – using his method later called Conductive Education. In 1938, Pető emigrated to Hungary and the Bobaths to Britain (Berta in 1935, Karel in 1939) as refugees. Berta Bobath began to work with a hemiplegic patient using her method in 1943 and obtained a diploma in physiotherapy in 1950. Her fellowship thesis was 'A study of abnormal postural reflex activity in patients severely affected with lesions of the central nervous system'. The Bobaths' pioneering work started in 1944 and they were joint founders of the Bobath concept. They started a private clinic in 1951, which became known in 1957 as the Western Cerebral Palsy Centre for children with cerebral palsy. They established a professional training system for teaching their fundamental concept, developed a mastery of training and assessment and trained whole generations. They ran introductory three-week Bobath courses. Both died on 20 January 1991, aged eighty-three and eighty-four.

Pető also worked with hemiplegic and paraplegic patients and those with other dysfunctions during the war and after. Pető's work was set up in Budapest in 1945 (earlier in Vienna). He was the founder of an institute in 1945 and became professor at the Special Education College in 1947 to teach his way of education. He received the State Institute for Movement Therapy in 1950 (later called the Institute for Conductive Education. and recently the International Pető Institute). Pető's institution became a college for professional education in 1963, offering degree-level courses. Pető died on 11 September 1967, on his seventy-fourth birthday.

In 1966 there was a Congress of the American Academy of Cerebral Palsy in New Orleans where Kabat, Rood, Deaver, Phelps, Doman and Bobath were invited to present papers on their different methods of treatment to the audience. On 16 January 1967 Berta Bobath wrote to Pető that they could not show anything but unsystematic techniques which had no effects on patients. Berta Bobath presented at the second International Symposium in Prague and mentioned Fay, Kabat, Brunstrom, Rood and also Pető's approach. She said the Bobaths were inhibiting abnormal patterns of posture and giving the child active control. About Pető's approach she said that he uses thoroughly planned patterns designed to stop abnormal ones, and mentioned the children's concentration and that the education extends throughout the week.

There are links between the approaches mentioned.

Similarities:

> cerebral palsy is viewed as a process (developmental);
>
> cerebral palsy is viewed as poor coordination (not a local phenomenon);
>
> controlled input (learned intention) is emphasised;
>
> inhibition, reduction of spasticity is achieved

Like all neurodevelopmental methods, both neurodevelopmental treatment and Conductive Education rely on the process of neurodevelopment – physiological and psychological – and rely on the fact that this process can be influenced. Dysfunction is not seen as a local muscular phenomenon, as in neurophysiologically based methods, and both Bobath and Pető viewed the CNS and the person as a whole. Difficulties were identified as poor, uncontrolled coordination. Differing from other neuro-developmental methods but similar to Alexander's and Feldenkrais's concepts, the Bobaths' and Pető's attention was focused on perceptual abilities, on central representation and the body image of action. Their ideas of controlled input were unique and similar. The final unique similarity is that the goal and result were relaxation, inhibition in both approaches.

The only difference is that the control of coordination is seen as a physiological process in one and as a cognitive process in the other approach. Therapy in one, education in the other.

In the Bobaths' neuro-developmental view the increase of postural tone and the upset of balance originate subcortically. Controlled input is achieved by reflex inhibition, reaction, response, below the conscious level, through positioning and handling, proprioceptive guidance from muscles, tendons, skin and vestibular sensors in individual treatment. In Pető's view development is a cognitive process. Controlled input is achieved whilst expecting the highest stage of brain activity of the person: active volitional acts are emphasised. Dysfunction is a cognitive learning problem, intention is significant, the patient is guided to find his own solution.

Bobath was right in that teaching movement is not good, functionalism reinforces spasticity, unconscious coordination cannot be directly learned. Those who think that they are using Conductive Education and describe what they are doing as preparation of functional skills – and speak about the purpose of motor activity – are misunderstanding Conductive Education. It is intention (without spasticity) that has to be learned, through conscious target-reaching which provides experience, sensation, memory and parametrisation. The teacher helps by education, through guidance and advice. Facilitation is also achieved by self-produced rhythm, dynamism and the group situation.

Concerning purposeful movement, recent neurophysiology has distinguished purposive movements from reflex movements, concluding that both achieve control of coordination, but guidance is given by handling in the one, and by a cognitive way in the other – by therapy in the one, by education in the other approach.

Because therapy and education are two different functions done separately, they are episodic. The programme is multidisciplinary not unified. Bobath stated:

> Indeed it was wrong to try to follow the normal developmental sequence too closely...charts of development...are unreliable for early diagnosis in the child with cerebral palsy, and even less use in assessment and planning of treatment...The last stage of the development of our treatment was the recognition of the fact that the treatment was not carried over into activities of daily life as we had expected it would be.[34]

The unified programme means that the same element which was learned is reproduced even when the activity is totally different, the same way in which grammar is learned. Taking account of the necessary purposeful action, the simultaneity of the action. (implying relaxation, posture, balance, skills in interconnection with emotional development, along with left-right differentiation, visual and spatial skills, face, tongue, breathing, articulation, vocalisation, language, intercommunication, attention, and academic skills) the key of the solution is conduction along a centrally coordinated programme, which requires a different expertise provided by special conductor-teacher training.

To conclude, Berta Bobath was an esteemed friend of Pető who included Bobath's theories in his own thinking and teachings. He

---

[34] Bobath, K. and Bobath, B. (1984) The neuro-developmental treatment. *In* Scrutton,D., ed. *Management of the motor disorders of children with cerebral palsy.* London: Spastics International Medical Publications, p.9.

wrote to the Bobaths that he was interested in them – that means in other words, he was interested in learning about their methods. Bobath's writings revealed similarity, difference and progress in her approach. She emphasised that over forty years she developed and changed her approach and emphasis, that is being neither rigid nor standardised, nor being dogmatic.

> Over the years we have been influenced by and have learned from other workers in the field. For example, we have learned from Knot (1952), Kabat and Knott (1953) and Knott and Voss (1973), and have recognised the importance of proprioceptive stimulation to build up tonus in patients with low and unstable postural tone. From Rood (1954) and Goff (1969, 1972) we have learned the value of tactile stimulation to obtain movements, especially of hands, feet mouth and tongue. We have learned most, however, from Pető (Cotton and Parnwell 1967, Clarke and Evans 1973) who, like us, saw that the problem for these children was inco-ordination of function, and this helped us better to prepare athetoid children for everyday life. We are still learning from our mistakes and omissions. [35]

Learning from others is nothing to be ashamed of. I think the greatness of people like Pető and the Bobaths begins in the openness, understanding, acceptance of new ideas. This is good for the welfare of children.

---

[35] Bobath,K., Bobath, B. (1984) The neuro-developmental treatment. *In* Scrutton, D., ed. *Management of the motor disorders of children with cerebral palsy.* London: Spastics International Medical Publications, p.8.

Neurodevelopmental treatment	Conductive Education
Physiological process, sub-cortical upset of balance	Cognitive process, highest stage of brain activity
Works below conscious level, reaction	Involves learning, volitional experience and acting purposefully
Uses reflex inhibition postural reflex activity through proprioceptive guidance, controlled input	Uses intention without spasticity and conscious control provided through conscious target-reaching
Therapist is positioning, handling	Conductor educates, gives guidance to self-produced rhythm, dynamism, positioning
Works with individuals	Uses groups
Uses multidisciplinary programme	Programme is unified, one discipline.
Therapy is interrupted by other services	Conduction is there throughout the day. Continuous learning through conduction, the expertise of the conductive educator

8.

Bowing out, 2000

This presentation in Birmingham in September 2000 was Mária Hári's swansong on the international stage. She was scheduled to appear at a further conference in London the following September but in the event was too frail to appear and her material was presented *in absentia* by PowerPoint. In the October she died.

In Birmingham in September 2000 she was in good spirits. She came with a travelling companion, Ilona Lázár-Péterné, a life-long friend since their days together at the Baar Madas School, Budapest's premier girls' high-school in the years before the Second World War, and the two spry elderly ladies treated it as a holiday. Contrary to her usual practice at conferences of sitting through everything, Mária Hári sat out sessions, talking to people who had known her, or went out walking in the city.

Though now frail she had maintained the old habit of rewriting and rejecting her prepared material. This paper is taken from the written paper that she brought from Hungary: in the event she spoke as she usually did, spontaneously, from notes written in her hotel room the night before. Though specifics varied, the under-lying message was the same. This typescript has already been edited and published[36]. It has been lightly edited again to bring it in line with the style of the rest of this collection.

Her theme is simple and wholly consistent with what she had hammered out in Hungary and beyond its boundaries right from when she took up Pető's mantle (we do not know what went before).

---

[36] *Recent Advances in Conductive Education*, 2(2), 2003, pp.80-85

The basic points as stated here are very simple.

Conductive Education is different

People have to understand how

Proper training is the key

Without this training there is only the simulation of Conductive Education, something different from Conductive Education even though bearing the same name. If something is truly Conductive Education, the orthofunctional spontaneity will permeate throughout the learner's whole life.

A year later, shortly before she died, she confided 'I was too rigid.' In this her last international presentation she lists some of the flexible generalisable principles of good conductive practice (she would call these 'metacognitive principles'). And she adds a final new perspective, the need for research bound in with the training and the practice.

She left exploration of this new theme not just to another occasion but also to others who would follow after.

András Pető's heritage

Paper presented at the Coming of Age conference,
Birmingham, 8-10 September 2000

We all are happy to be here because of our interest in Conductive
Education and wish to give information about our work and to get
information. I myself have the pleasure to be invited as the oldest
in Conductive Education, who first worked in 1945, and I accepted
and thank you for the invitation to this lecture as I appreciate that
Birmingham was after Japan the first to agree that the training of
professionals is essential.

I will say some words about the worth of this training, the worth of
the knowledge of this discipline. The reason why I want to speak
about the training is that the name given to my lecture is 'The
heritage of A. Pető', which is Conductive Education and the
training based on it. This *discipline* is not an addition or
combination of special disciplines. It has a special structure,
organization, content and training. The other reason is that while
doors have opened to Conductive Education one is not everywhere
armed with knowledge of it; greater understanding of this
discipline would help in that the overall way in which one thinks
about Conductive Education would actually correspond to
Conductive Education. The protection of the heritage would be to
provide greater understanding through excellent training for this
discipline.

The necessary profession

Conductive Education was not immediately known as a special
profession. To train the first special educators, in 1945 Pető got
two rooms at the special education institute to work with children
because some Hungarians knew that Pető can do better for
handicapped children and adults. These graduate students were
later directed back towards a more traditional form of training.
One did not want them to work in the way Pető planned.

One must know in what way one wants to work, this defines the training. From the very beginning Pető wanted to train professionals in his special way for learning to do the special educational work which Pető constructed. In Hungary it took twenty years till professionals were trained for this educational work, till this profession became accepted. Abroad it took thirty-two years till there was demand for training which provided Conductive Education in the original conception. Conductor training is now accepted in Japan, Birmingham, Israel, Keele/Scope, Russia and Spain. The training made it possible for those who executed the Pető programme with much help, to become professionals and work less aided and successfully. A post-graduate training is also recognised. Conductors are not bound to the soil: through their qualification they can work everywhere in the world. The term Conductive Education became known. This is development in a good direction.

A special way of education

In cases in which we are not willing to learn we use only a 'technique' to achieve rather a somewhat functional goal. This is a problematic situation, which could change with better understanding. I will explain its origin. The history of it is that Pető, the Institute and the Educational Ministry helped everybody who accepted help to work better. Later some who were helped to work better did not get the time and money to learn. The Alice in Wonderland logic is: 'We have a need, we don't see how to meet it, therefore we have no need.' They began to work, even to teach their own 'Conductive Education', but the initial help given was not enough, it led to misunderstanding, to using a few so-called task series as a 'special separate technique' in order to realise a rather functional goal. The term Conductive Education was used by them, and gained popularity as an umbrella term but there was a growing divide between Conductive Education and the umbrella Conductive Education. The provisions for children made by the leading authorities did not change. Half part of one child belonged to the education the other part to the health. This umbrella Conductive Education became used as a special physiotherapy within a multidisciplinary system to provide good function through an intensive program of exercises. The problem is that this behavioristical realisation of the set of actions of a good machine is an inaccurate conception and not the profession that should be provided. That means that one is really walking under a different umbrella.

Conductive Education's goal is to achieve orthofunctional spontaneity, (a) to convert intention into action and (b) to use this in every moment of our spontaneity in life.

Now you will ask me what is the heritage of A. Pető, what are the goals and the ways of a well planned unified programme. The goal is to learn a way of life, thinking, planning, a way of problem-solving, the ability to convert intention into action. It is to be found by the learner, who is conducted by the conductor who establishes activity and provides spontaneity, the precondition of problem-solving in the learner's whole life.

Most essential is to use the established way of activity in every moment of the learner's spontaneity in life. This purpose unifies the course of Conductive Education. It is central that you cannot know people partly – only their forenoon, from here to here. Pető was interested and you have to be interested in *all* factors of their life: he said 'I' does not exist, '*that*' exists. He was interested in maximal order outside and inside, it is a duty by extension of the sense that you may not say it is not my task to lift this peace of paper. This is a unique philosophy. It follows that every child's every minute must be planned, but at the same time every child must know that he is absolutely free to do what he wants and that he is the most essential, his skills are appreciated, his life has meaning.

The factors spontaneity and orthofunction must penetrate through the whole of life, unity must exist within a well planned unified programme. You can express it in two words: orthofunctional spontaneity (the term stems from Pető). To learn to realise this takes more than six years because, similar to metacognitive education, it is an open-system process.

Training in a special way

To make the trainee capable of realizing certain goals the trainee must learn not what to exercise but what to communicate and how? To realise any task given in a programme; how it is used to learn is special and individually different.

To realize suitable conductor-training one needs the following:

Observation. Learn to learn, the operative-observation way – this is a process, interactive and dynamic, it can go sideways and in any other way, it is fundamental to be capable to find the way in which somebody can do something that he cannot do, you do not await the result of some month-long exercise but you find the way immediately.

Repertoire. One needs acquaintance with the repertoire of several hundred ways, – if you are a composer, a Beethoven, you must know all the music compositions that have been made before.

Rules of composition. One needs the knowledge and realisation of Conductive Education's rules of composition, the fundamentals to communicate something through several levels, using emotional intensity, humour, human meaningfulness.

Realisation of complexity. The capacity to realise the law of complexity.

Coherence. The unity in the course of Conductive Education.

The dynamism, the connection. The atmosphere of active schools, through encouragement, personal educational dynamism, insight, creating connection.

The organization (the most difficult). Good organization is necessary.

Group leading. Special way of leading groups – big groups.

This all depends on the educators' attitude, their educational knowledge and skills. Learning this cannot be done just in verbal form. A best practice is needed. Theory alone, like watching a screen, kills conduction, makes blind, freezes.

Not to lose what I mean by heritage we need the best training: research, practice and training have to be unified.

In conclusion, I wanted to say that one can do things better, less better and one can do them totally differently: *any method may be effective but if we really want Conductive Education one has to provide the knowledge.* We must be sure to pass to the next generation what is the fundamental heritage of András Pető. I think we should be ready to:

> a)   on the one hand, accept help (that is a really good training), realising the academic, practical and educational preconditions; and
>
> b)   on the other hand , one should be ready, to offer this help.

Research, practice and training must be unified but this is a theme to explain for another occasion.

I hope my message may be welcome to many and think it should not be dismissed. I would be happy to know that in these things our opinions are in agreement. I wish to this conference to be successful and to help to a good development.

Her struggle continues

The contexts in which Mária Hári presented these papers are now history. Her cause remains. The need to communicate Conductive Education is as real today as it was when Mária Hári first spoke upon an international stage, in Wallingford in 1968. Conductive Education and its defining pedagogy *still* remain widely misunderstood – or ignored – and this demands far more study, systematisation and public explanation that the international conductive movement has yet to grant it. The context has changed and the question of how best to implement appropriate professional training persists in new forms and even the nature and identity of what constitutes 'a conductor' is subject to diverse and divisive debate. The claims of those who say 'we do that' and which entangled with Mária Hári's attempts to spread her own view of how best to implement András Pető's system have proved extraordinarily vigorous. And there is still the issue, rather differently expressed today, of 'making the statistic'.

Conductive Education around the world faces many practical hurdles for which there will be no single answer. Of those that Mária Hári addressed in the papers published here perhaps the first of these, the proper understanding of the essentially pedagogic nature of this way of working – and all that is implied by how this is 'conductive' – is perhaps the only and fundamental basis for addressing the others. Mária Hári may still prove to bring something important to this process but those who come after cannot expect the past alone to solve their problems. They have a responsibility to answer these questions themselves.

Index

A

admission criteria 51
adults 42, 92
Adult Conductive Education 13
aims 36-7, 41, 64, 78
aids 96
Ákos, K. 13, 56, 71
Ákos, M. 13, 71
algorithm 25-6, 36, 47
Alexander, F.M. 101
al-Khwarizmi, M. 25
assessment 89-90, 91, 99,
    102
    see also consultation
athetoid children 36, 37,
    38, 50, 75, 76, 77-80
atmosphere 35, 61, 112
attention 63
American Academy of Cerebral
    Palsy 100
audiologist 61, 90
asthma 57

B

Baar Madas School 105
Beethoven, L. 110
Belgium 17, 66
Berlin 99
Bernshtein, N.I. 69, 73, 74
Birmingham 19, 107, 108
Bobath method 65, 97
    compared with Pető's
    102-6
Bobath, B. 99, 102-3
Bobath, K. 97-8, 102, 103
Bobaths, the 97-8, 99-100,
    103
bond 31
Bounds, J. 11

Britain 82, 99
British Medical Journal 82-83,
    84, 87,
Bronfenbrenner, U. 26, 45
Brown, M. 13
Bruges 17
Brunstrom, S. 100
Brussels 19, 67, 75
Budapest 13, 17, 55, 57,
    81, 83, 100, 105, 107

C

Cambridge 19
Castle Priory College 17
    31, 33, 47, 57
cerebral palsy 42, 87, 90, 91,
    92, 100, 102, 104
Chailey Heritage Hospital
    81
children 42
Clarke, J. 103
Clifton, E. 11
cognitive 101
Cold War 85
Cole, M. 45
collective 35, 45, 50, 61, 80
College of Special Education
    (Budapest) 57
community 35, 45, 49-51
    58, 70
conduction 24, 72, 95-96, 111
Conductive Education 14
Conductive Education 33, 34, 3
    38, 40, 47, 48, 67, 81, 82, 87, 8
    92, 98, 99, 100, 104, 105-6,
    107, 108, 109, 111, 113
    aims/goals 41, 78, 111
    and pedagogy 45, 53, 60
    65-6, 69, 70, 71, 74-6
    criteria 34

115

characteristics 42-3
definitions 23-7
dissemination 19-22, 73, 81, 85, 109-10 113
history 55, 57-8
literature 13-14
as paradigm shift 97
as umbrella term 108-9
conductive examination 34 85
conductive observation 35-6, 39-42, 63
conductive pedagogy 13-4, 16, 18, 19, 34, 36, 45, 51
conductive upbringing 73 75, 77, 80
Conductor, The 73
conductors 35, 36, 39, 40, 48, 51, 61, 63-4, 72, 78, 82, 85, 88, 89, 95-6
  identity 57, 113
  in special institutions 89
  meaning 24
  outside Hungary 85
  repertoire 112
conductor-training 34, 43 53, 66, 67, 69, 102, 107-14
  as essential key 19, 72, 108
  for foreigners 19
  in Birmingham 13
  in Budapest 19, 41, 58, 102, 109-10
  requirements of 110-11
confidence 70
connection 31, 60
conscious 38, 45, 48, 49, 62, 95, 101
consultation 88-90
contact 15, 31, 34, 51, 70
contra-indications 89-90
coordination 70, 77, 78, 100-2
Cotton, E. 30, 31, 103

cortical function 45, 47
Czechoslovakia 19

D

daily programme 38, 40-1, 48, 60, 61, 67
Deaver, G. 100
Defektologya 73
Denmark 18
dentist 61, 90
Department of Education and Science, 35
dermatologist 90
development 27, 45, 75, 101, 102
Dina 14
Doman, G. 100
Dublin 18
dysarthia 60
dysfunction 25, 41, 42, 48, 50, 51, 57, 58, 60, 94, 101
dyskinesis 71

E

East Germany 85
emotions 34, 35, 70
England 13, 17, 19, 33, 66, 81
English language 14, 23, 30-1, 97
epidemiology 85
Evans, E. 103
excessive movements 78
experimental observation 35

F

facilitation 36, 39, 101
families 81
Fay, T. 100
feladatsor 25
Feldenkrais, M. 101

French language 15, 18-19, 26, 65
Foundation for Conductive Education 11, 19, 85
France 19
functions 70, 101, 108, 110

G

goals 62, 70, 71, 94, 95-6, 101, 109
Goff, B. 103
graduateness 13
groups 34-5, 45, 50-1, 58, 60, 64, 102, 111

H

habits 61
Hámori, M. 51
Hári, Mária
  biography 16-21, 97
  language 15-16, 30, 56
  photo 5
Hári-isms 15, 21, 27, 31, 83
Háriology 22
hearing difficulties 59
hemiplegia 42, 99
Hidegh, P. 51
History of Conductive Pedagogy 16
Holland 66
House, J. 31
Hungarian language 14, 30, 23-6
Hungarian People's Republic 17, 29, 30, 73
Hungary 13, 15, 18, 19, 20, 29, 81, 82, 83, 84, 90, 99, 105, 108

I

inclusion 22, 25
initiative 78
Institute of Defectology 73
intention 62, 78, 100, 101, 109
interest 37, 63, 70
International Cerebral Palsy Society 18
internist 30
Iron Curtain 81
Israel 108

J

Japan 19, 66, 108
joy 41

K

Kabat, H. 100, 103
kapczolat 31
Keele (university) 108
Knot, M. 103
Knowles, J.W. 30
konduktív nevelés 23
konduktív pedagógia 23-4
kondukció 24
konduktor 24
Korsakov Journal 74, 76
Kútvölgyi út 84

L

Lázár-Péterné, I. 105
Little, T.M. 80
London 105
Loring, A. 6, 18, 30, 53
Loring, J. 29-30, 53
love 31
  'intelligent love' 5
Ljubljana 97, 99
Luriya, A.R. 69

M

McCarthy, G.T. 80
McCracken, C. 82
McDowell E.Adobolyni 11
McGee, A-M. 11, 81, 83
McGuigan, C. 11
Maltzman, I. 45
Mastyukova, E. 71
Meadows, S. 26
Meldreth Manor School 29-30
Mikula-Tóth, Á. 14
Moscow 73
Motricité cérébrale 65
movement 35-43, 47-48, 52, 59, 63, 76-8, 94, 101-2, 113

N

National Institute of Conductive Education 13
National Library of Conductive Education 11, 14
nervous system 101, 103
neuro-opthalmologist 61
neuro-paediatric approach 65
nevelés 23, 26, 75
neurodevelopmental treatment 97. 99, 101, 104
neurologists 30
New Orleans 100
New Zealand 84

O

objective 94
observation
  see conductive observation
  see operative observation
obuchenie 26
Olmouc 18
operatív 24

operative observation, 24-5, 36, 95, 110
opthalmologists 90
orthofunction 25, 48, 94-5, 109
  orthofunctional sponteneity 106, 109
  see also dysfunction
orthofunkció 25
orthopaedic surgery 82
orthopaedist 61
Osaka 19
otorhinolaryngologist 90
outcomes 41-2, 51-3, 82
Oxford 18

P

paediatricians 61, 84, 90
paediatricians'course 84-5
paraplegic 42, 99
parents 80
Paris 19
Parnwell, M. 31, 103
part-functions 62
part-objectives 48
part-problems 47
Patrick, J. 86
pedagogy 18, 24, 60, 113
  see also conductive pedagogy
personality 49
Pető, András 13, 17, 20, 22, 29, 34, 55, 71, 97, 99, 100, 103, 105, 107, 108, 109, 111, 113
  and England 30
  and pedagogy 18, 19
  biography 57, 73, 99-100, 107-8
  heritage 16, 20, 109ff

Pető Institute 81, 82, 83, 84, 85, 87, 88, 92, 97
  International Pető Institute 83, 100
Pető method 67, 69, 95

Pető system 87, 88, 95, 96, 113
Phelps, W.M. 100
physiotherapy 82, 108
Poland 66
play 41
Prague 99, 102
'principles of Conductive
    Education' 13, 19
problem-solving 71, 109
programme *see* daily
    programme
psychologist 90

Q

qualitative change 47, 61, 96

R

Ram, M. 31
Read, J. 83
reafferentation 70, 75
*Recent Advances in Conductive
    Education*, 105
  refractive errors 60
repertoire 100
research 20, 34, 58, 106, 111
rhythm 102
Robinson, R.O. 80, 85, 90
Rood, M. 100, 103
Rózsahegyi, T
Russia 108
    see also Soviet Union
Russian language 15, 19, 26-7,
    74-5

S

San Marino 19
School for Parents 51
Scope 108
    see also Spastics Society
Scrutton, D. 103

second signalling system 39,
    43, 45
selectivity 84, 87-8
Semenova, K. 71
series of tasks
    see task series
singing 37
Slovenia 99
Soviet Bloc 73, 74, 75, 76
Soviet Union 73
    see also Russia
Spain 108
spasms 78
spasticity, 71, 100, 101
Spastics News 18, 30
Spastics Society 17, 29, 30, 55
    see also Scope
Special Education College
    (Budapest) 100
speech 37, 39, 48, 60, 77
spina bifida 87, 90, 91, 92
spontaneity 109
    see also, orthofunctional
    sponteneity
squints 60
Standing up for Joe 5, 81
State Institute 19, 20, 30, 34,
    49, 55, 57-8, 61, 73, 100
statistics 20, 27-8, 42, 52-3,
    58-9, 67-9, 79-80, 84, 90-4, 11
success 36, 37, 61, 63
supranuclear muscular
    imbalance 59
Sutton, A. 26
Suzdal' 23, 24, 26, 27, 73, 74,
    75, 76, 77
Szentesi, E. 11
Szombathely 99

T

task series 25, 36-9, 47-8, 71,
    72, 78, 108

tasks 35, 38, 39, 47, 61, 62, 63,
    71
therapeutic education 65
therapists 88, 97
therapy 97, 101, 102
Therapy Weekly 82, 85

U

United Kingdom 29, 31, 56, 83
    government support, 85
see also Britain
see also England
upbringing 23, 26
urologist 90

V

verbal accompaniment 71
Vienna 99, 100
Villanyi út 84
Vojta method 65, 97
vospitanie , 26, 75
Voss, D. 103
Vygotskii, L.S. 24

W

walking 25
Wallingford 6, 16, 17, 31, 33,
    45, 47, 55, 56, 57, 74, 113
Warashibe 19
Western Cerebral Palsy Centre
    99
will 62, 71, 78, 94
Wilson, J. 11
writing 38, 40-1

Other publications

Dina: A Mother Practises Conductive Education (English Edition)
Karoly and Magda Ákos
The Foundation for Conductive Education, 1991

This unique publication, appealing to parents and specialists alike provides
an insight into both the theoretical and practical approaches of Conductive
Education as a way of transforming young cerebral palsied children's
development. Through the correspondence between the authors and two
German mothers this book offers a fascinating illustration of how
Conductive Education can be used in everyday life.
Price: £11.95

Adult Conductive Education
M. Brown and A. Mikula Toth
Stanley Thornes Publishing Ltd, 1997

Written by the Foundation's conductors, Melanie Brown and Agnes
Mikula Toth, this is the first textbook to focus on Conductive Education
for adults with motor disorders. Adult Conductive Education is an
informative text that offers insight into the nature and philosophy of
Conductive Education and outlines the underlying principles that are often
not well understood.
Price: £18.50

Recent Advances in Conductive Education
This journal covers practical issues in the field with contributions from
those interested in and working towards the development of Conductive
Education worldwide. It is published twice a year, June and December.

Further details about these and other publications from

Publications
National Institute of Conductive Education
Russell Road
Moseley
Birmingham, B13 8RD
UK

library@conductive-education.org
www.conductive-education.org